Partnership Foundations

By David Carr, Chris Beard, Hilary Beard, Niall Cluley,

David Insull, Anne Lowe and Justin Marsh

First Edition February 2006

Renewal Christian Centre

Partnership Foundations

Authors: David Carr, Chris Beard, Hilary Beard, Niall Cluley,

David Insull, Anne Lowe and Justin Marsh

First Edition February 2006

Published in China

© Renewal Christian Centre 2006

All rights reserved. No part of this publication may be reproduced, transmitted or stored in a retrieval system in any form without the prior written permission of Renewal Christian Centre, Lode Lane, Solihull, West Midlands, England, B91 2JR.

Published by 8E Media Ltd
Creative Industries Centre
Wolverhampton, England

Printed in China

www.renewalcc.com

Preface

Back in 1984 the Founder & Senior Pastor of Renewal Christian Centre, Reverend Dr. David Carr, asked me to take over responsibility for looking after the new Christians at Renewal. Part of this responsibility involved taking the New Christians' Bible Study once a week, using a set of notes which had been used by my predecessor. While these notes were fine, I felt lead of the Lord to write my own, alternative course and so approached Pastor David for his permission to do so; this he duly granted and so was "born" the first of the courses Renewal has used ever since to teach new Christians the basics of the Christian faith. This course has been through a number of versions, reflecting in part the launch of our own in-house Church-based Bible School - currently known as the Renewal Bible Training Centre - in 1988, and also the introduction to Renewal some years ago of the successful Alpha course, first pioneered in Holy Trinity, Brompton. During 2004 the Directors of the Renewal Bible Training Centre decided to update our course for new Christians once again and this resulted in a 6-week course entitled *Partnership Foundations.*

In devising this course we had in mind the need to explain to folk attending Renewal how the Church had been founded and then to give them some of the key factors in its growth over the years. In addition, we decided to give foundational Bible-based teaching on some of the key issues, or doctrines, in the Christian faith in order to better equip believers to walk by faith and also to share their faith with others.

It is our belief that the concepts and truths contained in these notes are not specific and exclusive to Renewal, but are of value to Christians from other churches and denominations. Hence the decision to make them available via this book.

Ever since I first began writing Bible teaching notes back in 1984, I have relied heavily on the ideas and inspiration that the Holy Spirit has given to other teachers and writers in the Christian Church. I have always tried to acknowledge the assistance I have received from them, not least by giving a list of sources used in the preparation of the notes. As always I am deeply indebted to those people, but also to countless other preachers, teachers and writers who have influenced my thinking and faith over the years since I became a Christian.

I would like to mention in particular two people who have been instrumental in assisting me in the work I have done in the Renewal Bible Training Centre since 1988. First, Pastor David Carr who first asked me to get involved in Bible teaching and who took the decision to ask me to take charge of the Renewal Bible Training Centre when it was started all those years ago, and who has supported me in that role ever since. He has been a loyal and faithful supporter, as well as a regular and willing teacher himself. Without doubt the Renewal Bible Training Centre would not have developed as it has if he had not made such a huge contribution to it over the years; for one who is so busy in other ways, this has been a tremendous commitment and we are all most grateful to him.

Second, I would like to thank my wife, Jean, whose unstinting support, help, advice and hard work have contributed so hugely to all that we have managed to do in the Renewal Bible Training Centre. Most of what she has done has been "behind the scenes" and so largely unnoticed by others. However, her contribution has been vital and I am keen that more public recognition be given to her enormously important role and work.

I trust that those who read this book will not find any errors; however, should you do so, please accept my apologies, as I take full responsibility for them. I do hope that all who read this book will find its contents a blessing and that they will be encouraged in their faith and in their walk with the Lord Jesus Christ. To Him be all the glory!

Niall Cluley,
December 2005.

Contents

Chapter		Page
Introduction		1
1	The Origin Of Renewal	3
	The Concept Of Partnership	14
2	What It Means To Be A Christian	19
	Water Baptism	24
3	Introduction To Cells	27
4	Finance, Giving & Stewardship	45
5	Ministry Opportunities & Serving	65
6	Holy Communion	93
	Renewal's Leadership Structure	101

Introduction

The "Partnership Foundations" course was introduced into Renewal in 2005 and is intended primarily as information for those considering whether or not to join Renewal as new partners. However, anyone can attend this course, which is provided free by Renewal's Bible School, known as the Renewal Bible Training Centre (RBTC). The course takes place on Thursday evenings between 7.30 and 9.45 p.m. and all are welcome. The dates on which the course will be held are advertised widely within Renewal. Each attendee at the course receives this book of notes. The contents of the 6-week course are:

Week Number	Content
1	The Origin Of Renewal
	The Concept Of Partnership
2	What It Means To Be A Christian
	Water Baptism
3	Introduction To Cells
4	Finance, Giving & Stewardship
5	Ministry Opportunities & Serving
7	Holy Communion
	Renewal's Leadership Structure

The notes for Week 1 are based on tape recordings made by David Carr in 1998 and 2004 and were typed by Joyce Deeming & Yvonne East.

The notes for Week 2 were written and typed by Hilary Beard and Anne Lowe.

The notes for Week 3 were written and typed by Justin Marsh.

The notes for Week 4 were written and typed by Chris Beard; the appendix is based on tape recordings made by David Carr in 1998 and were typed by Joyce Deeming.

The notes for Week 5 were written and typed by Hilary Beard; the appendix is based on tape recordings made by David Carr in 1998 and were typed by Joyce Deeming.

The notes for week 6 (Holy Communion) were written and typed by David Insull, while the notes re Renewal's Leadership Structure were written by Niall Cluley & David Carr.

Niall Cluley edited the notes for all 6 weeks.

These notes may not be reproduced in part or in total without the prior written permission of: The Principal, RBTC, Renewal Christian Centre, Lode Lane, Solihull, West Midlands, B91 2JR.

These notes were produced in this format in 2004.

Scripture quotations in these notes and lectures, unless otherwise stated, are from the Holy Bible, New King James Version, Copyright 1982, 1980, 1979 by Thomas Nelson, Inc. and are used by permission.

WEEK 1
ORIGIN OF RENEWAL

THE CONCEPT OF PARTNERSHIP

(These notes consist of the transcripts of two tape recordings made by the Senior Minister, Pastor David Carr, in 1998; on pages 13 - 17 is a further section - provided in 2004 - updating this information)

Welcome

Welcome to the Renewal Christian Centre, Solihull. My name's David Carr, I am the Senior Team Minister here. We are putting on some courses to which we invite you to listen. There are so many people joining the Church at the moment from all round the world and many parts of England that we feel it's good to understand where we've come from, what we believe and what we believe partnership really is, both for you and for the fellowship.

Therefore, we want you to sit back, listen, get the Word of God open and we trust as we go through this series that you will be blessed. If there are any questions you want to share with a Pastor we are available. May the Lord bless you!

The Origin of Renewal Christian Centre

Now our first study today is 'Where did the Church come from?' - the history of the Church. The Church started in 1972. What happened was at that time I was an evangelist travelling round the country preaching and had a worship band and we were seeing God doing incredible things. We saw people healed and people saved and we travelled in 23 different denominations. I was not a denominational man even though I had been born again in an evangelical Church. I was baptised in water in an Assemblies of God Church. I was filled with the Holy Spirit in an Assemblies of God Church, but I was an evangelist moving throughout all the different denominations.

Then in 1972 I remember driving into Solihull, which was only 7 miles from where I lived and I just wondered why there wasn't a Spirit-filled Church in the town. The town comprised a population of 90,000 and in the whole borough it's 200,000 and there were many fine Churches there, really good Churches that preached the Word of God, but there wasn't one that was given over to the gifts and the works of the Holy Spirit.

I remember standing in the town arguing with God. You see evangelists are often quite arrogant; we reap where other people sow and we tend to think that all we've got to do is turn up and wonder why all the crowds aren't waiting for us. I remember saying to the Lord, "You should really open a Church in this town, there is no Spirit-filled witness", and it was almost as if I could hear the voice, the Lord said to me, "If you are so concerned, you do it". And I said, "No, I am an evangelist, I am not a pastor. I go round preaching and praying for the sick". And the Lord said, "You do it". I was driving round a place called Solihull Lodge and I saw a Community Centre just being built and it looked very much like a Church and then I was foolish enough to say to God, "That would make a good Church, someone should start one there". With that the Lord said, "You start one".

Now I didn't know anybody in Solihull save one lady, I didn't know where she lived, I didn't know anything about her other than I had met her at a Church once and she said she was from Solihull. Our problem is that when we ask God for the impossible, He is the impossible God. I said, "If you want me to start a Church in Solihull, then as I get into my car and I drive round the corner I want to meet that lady". You know we shouldn't test God because when He answers there's no way out; so I got in the car, drove round the corner and - you are ahead of me now - she was there. In fact, she waved me down. She had got a shopping bag in one hand and she wound the window down. She said, "What are you doing in Solihull?" I said, "I'm just driving through" and she said to me, "Well, they are building a Community Centre round the corner"; she said, "You should start a Church there". So, I quickly wound the window up and drove home, but I couldn't get this out of my mind and out of my heart and then God gave me a Scripture from Timothy that said this, **"First of all pray for those who are in authority over you and for kings that you might have a peaceful life. I have ordained you that you may cause men to lift holy hands unto the Lord"** and I just knew that God was telling me that I had got to come and establish a work in this town.

I didn't know anybody, again evangelists they start something, they don't finish it, and it's a different gifting. So I managed to find out who operated the Community Centre and a Committee with a Chairman ran it and I phoned him up and I said, "I just wondered what would be the possibilities of hiring this Centre when it opens as a Church". "Oh", he said, "there's going to be a Church". I said, "What do you mean"? He said, "we have 7 Churches who have already asked to use it" and he said "the one that we have given it to is - I don't know what it is, it's called the Assemblies of God". "Oh", I said, "that is fantastic". He said, "the second one is the Jehovah's Witness and the third one on the list is Mormon" and he was going all the way down the list. And I said, "that's fine, that's wonderful" and the Lord said, "No, it's not, ask him to put your name on the list". So, I said, "would you put my name on the list"? and he said, "where are you from"? And I told him and he said, "what denomination are you"? I was an evangelist, I was worshipping at an Elim Church, which is a Pentecostal Church, but I wasn't in a denomination. Then he said, "What are your fundamental beliefs"? I hadn't got any. So I hadn't got anything to send him to show I was accredited, but he still put my name on the list. So I put the phone down and I said to the Lord, "Well, Lord" - I felt quite smug really, I thought, God I have been obedient, I have done everything You told me to do. Now Lord, You just wanted to test my obedience; the Assemblies of God, who are a fine denomination, they are already there: I'm safe, thank you Jesus, I can go back now to evangelising.

A few days later the Lord came to me again: "I want you to start a Church in Solihull" and I said, "Lord we've been through this before" and then I gave my next test of God and I said, "If you want me to pastor that Church, then by tomorrow at 12.55 in the afternoon they are going to phone my house and they are going to give me that building"; and I went away saying, "Get out of that one God, I've got you now"!

Aren't we terrible the way we test God? And the Lord said, "You know, try Me". I really did, I was very trying. I came home at night and forgot all about it and came to the door at 6 o'clock and suddenly remembered. I said to Molly, my wife, I said, "Did anybody phone today"? She said, "No". Thank you Jesus. "Oh, no", she said, "I made a mistake, there was. Somebody phoned up - the Chairman of the Community Association wants you to phone him back". I said, "What time did he phone"? She said, "I don't know, it's not that important is it"? I said, "It's important". So I phoned him back, a man called Mr Golding, and I said to him, "David Carr", and he said "Mr Carr"; I said, "Yes". He said, "A funny thing happened yesterday. The Assemblies of God phoned us up and said they don't want the building any more. They don't want to start a Church in Solihull". He said, "The Jehovah's Witnesses are next, but I don't know why I have done this and I have had a chat with the Committee and I want you to start a Church in Solihull". I think he expected me to explode with gratitude, but I didn't want to be a Pastor, never wanted to be a Pastor. I said to him, "Could you tell me what time you phoned my wife?" and he said "What time I phoned your wife? Why"? I said, "I just need to know". "Well", he said, "Let me think. Oh", he said, "It was just before 1 o'clock because I heard the pips go for the news when I put the phone down. Why, is that important"? I said, "Yes".

So I got to the point where I stopped struggling. God said He wanted me to start a Church, so what I did was I put a lot of leaflets through doors and got some friends from Churches to do that. Didn't know what to expect. Borrowed some hymn books, had no pianist, just my wife and myself and I had got two years bookings for evangelism, so I knew I was only going to start the Church and be there for a few weeks, because I was God's mighty man of power and why waste me in Solihull Lodge?

God changes you doesn't He and so just before the opening service on August 11th 1972, I put an ad in the newspaper about the opening of a new Church. It was called Trinity Free Church, that's what we called it at that time. The local paper phoned me up and said, "What's this new Church?" and so I told them. I didn't tell them about the tests, I thought no way am I telling you about this, this is weird. I didn't tell about God cancelling all the others (who wanted the building), I just said that I felt that we were not better than the rest but slightly different and did all this.

I bought the paper on Saturday - all over the front page, "Churches say get out, we don't want you", and they had phoned all the other Churches up and said, "What do you think of another Church coming into the town"? and they said, "We don't need them", which, in one sense, is true, as there has never been a redundant Church in Solihull, and one of the Churches (in the town) had really run us down (in the newspaper).

A young couple had just moved to Solihull because God had told them to give up their teaching jobs in Slough and to come to Solihull and to become teachers. They didn't know where Solihull was and they sat in Mell Square with no job and they are not that type of people, no home and no hope, not knowing why they are there. They buy a paper to see if there is any accommodation they can afford to rent until they get established and they saw this big furore about me in the front page: Get out of town, this town is not big enough for about twenty of us. Oh, they said, that looks a good Church, so that Sunday they went to the Church of their denomination and they told me afterwards that they thought if this is life and they are attacking this other guy than perhaps the other guy has got life. So they just phoned me up from the advert and they said I just want to ask you this question, what do you believe? I told him what I believed and he said we'll be with you on Sunday. That was a man called Geoff and Althea Greenaway and that was 26 years ago and they have been with me ever since. They were the first people to come into the Church so the Church was started with 4 people and you make lots of mistakes in life.

We had this little place and I said to the Lord in an arrogant way, any person who can't have between 100 - 150 people in their Church isn't fit for the ministry, as I had preached to hundreds and thousands and you pretend to think it's so easy you just go there and preach and dozens come out at the altar call.

One year later I had 12 in the Church. I remember the Lord saying to me one day, He said, "Son", I said, "Yes, Lord". "I have just come for your resignation". I said, "Why"? He said, "You've only got 12 and you said you're not fit"; and I said, "Lord, perhaps I was a little rash". He said, "No, you are a little arrogant". He said, "You know you're not going to reap what you've not sown, but they that sow in tears will reap with joy". Then we went to the dizzy heights of 25, made up mainly of old people and broken people and slowly people would come in and we would have some good times.

It was so cold in the winter we would sit round the kitchen, put all 4 rings on to keep warm and I would go home and it seemed so strange; I was used to preaching to hundreds, but I would go home all excited and say to Molly, "We had 8 in tonight". She said, "8, wow we've grown". "Oh, love it's been great". Eight, there were so many in tonight that we opened the oven to let the heat come out! Wow! We had to go round and pick them up and drive them home and lock the building. This was far short of being God's man of power for the hour!

And we continued like that and then my son, when he was born, my wife said "Rush me into hospital" and we went to the Birmingham Maternity Hospital and I got a book to read. It was very hard being an expectant dad: you know you go through a lot of pain, suffering and grief, and it was a man called Pink writing on Elijah, a great writer. I got my book in my hands as my wife's going through the contractions and I'm saying, "Don't shout so loud love, I'm reading" and as I'm reading this he shares how Elijah, who is a great man of power for the hour, has been brought into a desolate place with just a stream and the stream dried up. Then he had to be fed by birds having raw meat and you know we often eulogise over the Bible stories, but for a man to take food from a bird's beak when it's raw chunks of meat, you've got to be desperate. You've got to be desperate. Men wouldn't do that. It's a filthy thing to have to do; yet he was so hungry that he ate. He was even more humiliated, he had to go to a widow who had even less than he had and ask her to give everything she had got and God showed me there it was not because God was trying to humiliate him, God was trying to humble him. There is a big difference. Humiliation comes through Satan and through sin. Humbleness is the pre-requisite to be used of God and so I was going through that and God said to me this, He said, "Listen, you are a young preacher, you are full of self and you are full of the power; what would you do if I told you to stop in Solihull for the rest of your life? If you never ever preached at another rally and you never took another crusade and you never saw anybody saved and you never saw anybody healed again, would you sit here in the wilderness with these 25 people? If I asked you to do that would you do that? Would you do that"? I sat there in that delivery room and I said, "Lord if you want me to pastor 25 people for the rest of my life I count it a privilege". There was no flash of lightning, there was no thunder, there was no voice saying, "this is my son in whom I'm well pleased", but something changed in my heart, and then in the next couple of months we went to 60.

What God was saying is, while they are your sheep and they are your converts and why it's your vision, I can't get in, but are you prepared to let Me in so that it's My Church? See God never told us to go build Church, He said go & preach kingdom. Jesus said, **"I will build My Church and the gates of hell shall not prevail against it"**, and so often we run round building Church when we are here to preach kingdom. If we preach the kingdom and we are finding this over the last few months as we've been going straight down the line with the Gospel, going back to preaching the "red bits" as I call them, what has happened is that God is building His Church. We are beginning to grow and miracles are happening amongst the people, which we can't tell so much of because they are very personal and private things that are happening, but God is building His Church. I think it's far easier when God builds the Church, because when He builds it you can be sure He knows what He is doing. We preach the kingdom,

God builds the Church. It's a hard lesson that some of us never learn all our lives; many preachers spend all their lives trying to build a Church. Jesus said, "I'll build My Church" and He said to Peter, "I'll build one on you as well". You know God can build it on whom He likes, but it's His Church. I just found a contentment.

During that time I was still booked up and so I didn't want a Church to be built on a man and knowing it was an independent work we changed the name then to Trinity Pentecostal Church. We suddenly come out of the closet and said we were Spirit-filled and that frightened some more off, but some more came and we had people starting to get wonderfully touched by God. I just felt the Church needed the protection of aligning with a group of Churches, so that God moved me on back into evangelism which I always believed He would and prayed He would that they would be able to find a Pastor to come alongside them and not be left in a void with no Pastor. So I examined four or five different denominations and groupings and we finished up joining the Elim Pentecostal Church, which is very similar to the Assemblies of God and then I studied for five years and was ordained by them in 1978 and became a Minister of theirs, but still had this interdenominational concept and those of you who come to this Church, you won't really know if we are denominational or not because we preach the kingdom of God, we are not ashamed of being Pentecostal, but we don't preach that as the salvation of the world.

I could easily be a Methodist or I could be a Baptist or I could be anybody. Because, it's the Word of God that's real; it doesn't matter what your denomination is. It matters not what your denomination is; it's, "Are you preaching the Word and is the Word alive"? No one grouping or Church can change you; it's the living God. Now since that time I have preached in more than 23 denominations. I preach in all the major streams in the Pentecostal tradition, the charismatic, the faith and by God's grace they accept me in every one of them as one of their brothers. So, that's the mark of relationship that if you are accepted by the Word and not by your grouping. So, when people, young people leave our Church and go to University, we say join the Church that's hearing from God, don't worry about the label. Go to a Church that's hearing from God, that's all that really matters.

So we ambled along; I then started cancelling a lot of my bookings and spending more time in the town and the Lord said to me one day, "Ask Me questions". I said, "What questions"? He said, "Ask Me, are you going to stay in this building"? I said, "Am I going to stay in this building"? He said, "No". With 60 people, God gave me a vision that day and it's never changed. People who have heard this and this explanation said it's never changed in all those years. God said there will be 5,000 people in your fellowship. He said you are going to have worship bands, music bands. He showed me everything we were going to have and from that time I knew exactly what God wanted, but I thought it was going to happen next week, next year, maybe two, maybe three. I didn't realise that 25 years on we would be nowhere near it yet!

A lot of people come in and say, isn't it great, a blessed Church, God's working and I say hallelujah! We had on Sunday a thousand people through the Church and we used to have 500 people through the Church and we were 10% of the vision, now we are a fifth. I do believe that by God's grace this vision of 5,000 can be met very shortly. People are going to get born again and changed in a miraculous way, healed. We are going to see things happen which will bring glory to God. We have got to keep up with God, that's what's going to be happening.

The Lord said to me, "Test Me". I thought, what are we going to do, we are right on the outskirts on the borders of Birmingham and very quickly what I did I just prayed and prayed and couldn't get direction. I didn't know what was happening, so I booked a week's mission right in the North side. I took a week's mission where we were and then I booked the Civic Hall, which is the biggest auditorium in the town, which cost a lot of money which we hadn't got and I did a week there and the week there was to start on Sunday, October 13th at 8 o'clock at night, everything against us. Nobody has a night meeting in Solihull. Nobody does it on October 13th because they are all superstitious and you don't do at 8 o'clock when everybody is going home. So we went there and went into the big auditorium and I said my faith didn't rise to the 1,000 seater. So I said what's the next, so they said 350. Now you have got 60 people and I am booking this for a week and I said we'll have that. Now I got all the members of the Church and I made them team and I sent them into all the various parts and I went there and I got the preacher in who was a friend of mine and I said right we are going to go for it and we are praying here at 7.50pm. I thought Oh God, Oh God what have I done? I have got all this place, I can't pay for it. I've got all this place and I can't fill it and God said, "Test Me. Test Me and see". So at 7.55 p.m. I stand up on the platform feeling absolutely vulnerable and I peep through the curtain and it's packed and we saw people saved and healed who are still in the Church today. God really moved.

God said, "Right now I want you in the middle of Solihull". I tried everywhere and couldn't find a place and then one of my team, I asked him to come and be my Assistant Pastor because we were up to about 100 now and he said, "No, no I am not going to come, God has told me to be a teacher" and one night he went to bed and he said he saw a vision of a building with a parquet floor. It was made as a Sports Stadium and he saw it filled with people with the wind rushing in, with people with their arms raised and God said, "Go to Solihull". He phoned me up and it didn't mean a thing to me. Two weeks later the United Reformed Church, which is at the top of Seven Star Road, phoned me up and said, "We don't have a Sunday night meeting, do you want to come and look at our building and see if you want to hire it?" I went there, the Minister said to me, "We won't go through the front door, we will go through the back door" and as we come into the worship centre I freeze because it was a parquet floor made out for badminton. I said, "We'll have it." He said, "I haven't told you how much." I said, "We'll have it."

We were there 8 years and we saw exactly that happen. We were in that building and if you weren't there by 6.15pm for 6.30pm you didn't bother to come. It held about 220 people, it was packed. People were sitting on the widow ledges. I saw a cancer go from a woman's throat. We had somebody brought in on a stretcher and they were raised and walked out. We saw God move in miraculous ways. I would be preaching, sometimes and a gold aura was all round me. The presence of God was mighty. We saw people going down under the power of the Spirit before we ever knew what it was. The first time somebody went down in the power of the Spirit was my keyboard player's wife. I stopped the meeting and said, "Excuse me, she has fainted." We looked and she was smiling while she was fainting and we suddenly found it was the power of God. God just used to sweep round and take people out all over the place. We suddenly found we had revival in a school, and I mean revival. We had Christian Unions there at lunchtime and found them queuing all round to get into the room. We had to have 3 Christian Unions at the school of a night time and we had 70 girls from the grammar school get born again, Spirit filled and coming to the Church. They became our Youth Department. They never wanted to play ball, they never wanted to play anything. All they wanted to do was to sit there, read the Bible, worship and praise God in unknown tongues. We just had revival.

God was doing incredible things and right at the height of it some men came to me one day and said, "You know Pastor Dave, people are only coming to see the miracles. People are saying they are going to Dave Carr's Church"; and I thought, Oh my goodness and they said, "We know. We know that you didn't really want that. You see they should be given the solid Word. They shouldn't just be coming for the miracles". I said, "What do you suggest?", being naïve you see. They said, "If you stand back for 3 months and let us preach the solid meat then we will see whose here for the miracles".

I remember that Sunday I sat back in these big high chairs and the Lord said to me, "So you save them do you"? I said, "No". "So, you heal them do you"? I said, "No". "Well, if you can't cope with the anointing I've given you, I am going to take it off you. I am going to scatter this faithless generation". Within one year, most of them had gone and God took His anointing off me and for the next 2 years I preached without any sense of God at all. By pure obedience to God. He withdrew Himself from me altogether and it was just as if a cloud went by and 2 years later He turned round and said, "Will you listen to Me now"? I said, "Yes, please God". He said, "I'm going to give you a prophetic Word now, you couldn't handle the rest. I'm going to give you a profound word of knowledge now. Now don't abuse that". I found that people would be walking in and coming in and I turn round and be able to give them times and dates and seasons and God started doing a great thing and the Church grew and God brought Team Ministry in, then we bought a school in 1982.

That was a miracle of God. God said, "Offer £120,000" - well below value - and we got it. We outgrew that. God expanded a team; I had Pastors come in from New

Zealand and Africa. They have gone and gone back to their countries and we grew again and on the way to South Africa one day God said to me, "You have got to move into the Town Hall". That was a £1,000 a Sunday. I said to my administrator, who was on his way to Johannesburg with me, we were preaching at Rhema, I said, "Hey, God's just said, we've got to book the Town Hall, a 1000 seater". That was big faith, so we phoned them up and they said we could have it and so we started in the Town Hall. We started to grow again and God started doing great things again and I could keep you here all night trying to tell you 26 years of miracles, savings, healings, deliverances, like you would not credit. God really beginning to bless people and then He led us to this place - and the place that we meet in now was a factory just a few years ago. We bought that; it's now worth about £2 million. We have a £300,000 mortgage, which we believe in God we are going to wipe that out in two or three years and we don't believe we should be in any debt. We are going to wipe that out and build a big 5,000 or 6,000 Family Centre. Church isn't the building, it's the people and God has given us the strategy that we will spread throughout the Midlands with a Church in the Heart of England.

We are going to have communities all round the place and we are going to spread and become the Church in the street, the Church in the community. History is still being written, God is still doing good things, God put us here right on the main road; we are having people walking right into the Church.

God said a few weeks ago, "In five years I am going to bring people from all round the nation to your Church". Now Solihull is not a cosmopolitan area. It's not an area where people come from all round the world. We are a commuter city for Birmingham and the church were Caucasian white, we had only one black person in the Church and suddenly in the last five a prophet came in from Australia and said, "God said, you are going to be multi-racial and you are going to impact the whole nation from here".

Now we have 28 nations in the Church and they are coming in from all over the place and God is bringing mature Christians to us for such a time as this. God is sending people of faith to join us, He is sending people of experience, He is sending people of vision from all round the globe. Then God said only a few weeks ago, "I want you to buy a flag for every nation and I want you to put flags up: I am the Lord Your healer, I am Your provider, Royal Priesthood, King of Kings, Lord of Lords, Love your neighbour as yourself, the God of our salvation" and He said, "As you put those up I am going to bring more people in from the nations and everything that I have put on those banners I will do". We put them up and people are still coming in from around the world and only just this week we had an incredible Prayer Meeting as people stood under everyone of those banners according to their need and the power of God hit them. People told me afterwards that as I prayed from the platform they felt the power of God hit them as they stood under the banners. **"He brought me into His banqueting house and His banner over me is love".**

So, God is doing great things. He is a miraculous God and I trust that in this brief explanation of our history, even though I've left a lot out, will have shown you that. One day we will write a book about it, but God is into changing the lives of people. Yes, we meet in a building, but God knows what He is doing. Twenty-six years ago God gave me a vision when I lay on my bed, in fact it was thirty years ago, "Will you nurse my black babies"? I struggled, being an ex-bouncer I didn't think nursing was a man's job, and I saw myself all in white nursing this black baby. I struggled and went down to a local hospital and they said to me I could do nurse training. At the last minute I withdrew and thought it was a false vision. All of my life I had wanted to go to South Africa, but had never been there. I had a missionary over there from our Church and I was at a big conference and bumped into a man I hadn't seen for 12 years and God told me at 10 o'clock I was going to Rhema (church in South Africa), I was going to South Africa. I went into a big room and bumped into someone I hadn't seen for 12 years, his name was Gordon Kalmire, and he said, "Do you go abroad now"? I said, "I am going in June to South Africa". He said to me, "Who's doing your itinerary"? I said, "The Holy Spirit. God only told me 10 minutes ago, Gordon". He said, "Come see my boss". He took me through a room and there was a man called Ray McCauley (Senior Pastor, Rhema Church, South Africa) there. "Pastor Ray, this is my friend Dave Carr" he said, "Really love him, he is relevant. He said he is coming to South Africa and he doesn't have an itinerary". Ray said, "He has now. Book him". I came out of that room and in twenty minutes I'd had the vision of God to go to Africa and all my booking done.

I was at a Conference a few weeks later when a man came in with a young man with long hair and he said, "This is the man you were cursing". I said, "What are you on about"? He said, "This is a story"; he said, "This young man, who was demon possessed, walked into an evangelical Church and started manifesting. They didn't know what it was, thought he had a fit and took him to hospital. The doctor at the hospital came out and said, 'is this man from Africa'? They said, 'no'. 'Has he been there'? They said, 'no'. 'Does he know languages'? They said, 'no'. He said, 'he is speaking in my South African dialect and he is cursing a man called David Carr and he is saying, we will not have him in our country'. They then realised he was demonic, took him to this Pentecostal Pastor who got him delivered, saved, filled with the Spirit, and now he walks in and says, "this is the man you have been cursing". God said, "I have to keep doing this to you son because you are so thick you never realise when I'm asking you to do something. Go to South Africa"; and I have been there for many years now and then God said, "I'm going to take you round the world" and I have never had to ask for an invite to any country. Every time God has put a country on my heart, e.g. Ireland, he's done that. But when I was in South Africa after 24 years of having that vision I was asked to preach in Soweto. I went to Soweto and they wouldn't receive me. I was white, I was English and didn't know their culture and right in the middle of it the Holy Spirit said to me, "Ask the Pastor if you can bless the children". The Pastor was amazed; they bought those black children to me, some lovely, some dirty and I held them and kissed them and the power of God came upon us. God broke out, people got saved and delivered as they wept all over me, this white man who loved and held their babies who kissed and cuddled them. As I was coming out of Soweto, where there is a permanent smog over it, as I am coming out suddenly God relays the video of me nursing His babies and I looked and wept because I was dressed all in white. God said, "Today you nursed My babies".

I want to say that if we are a Church that loves God, a Church that loves vision, it's so easy to mistake what God is saying, but the Bible says, **"Hear what the Spirit is saying to the Church"**. As you begin to find out the various facets of our belief then I trust you'll realise that we are not the perfect Church. We have not made it, we have not arrived. I trust the arrogance that I had as a young man has gone and if it hasn't, God may You take it; but I will tell you that after being here twenty six years we can do all things through Christ as our strength but we can do nothing in our own strength.

I trust you'll enjoy these sessions and if you want to know more about us, more about our history, just catch any Pastor and we would love to come and see you. God bless you.

Update (produced in 2004)

Change from Elim to Free Methodist

The church commenced in 1972. Pastor David believed that a church should not be autonomous but should identify itself with an authority and covering and therefore joined the Elim Pentecostal Church Incorporated in 1974. Elim ordained Pastor David in 1978 and the church continued in fellowship with them until 2003 with Pastor David serving as a member of the Executive.

In 2002 Pastor David was challenged to 'help to open up Wesley Wells' which would facilitate another move of God in our nation. After much prayer and discussions with the Elim Pentecostal Church, Pastor David and the Elders submitted themselves to the vulnerability of such a call, and joined the Free Methodist Church of North America and the UK in January 2003.

The Free Methodist Church is a fine movement, which was started 143 years ago by Methodist Pastors, and men who had been filled with the Holy Spirit and would not allow wealth, race or inhibiting the Holy Spirit to prejudice the gospel message. They therefore formed the Free Methodist Church, which is now represented in 63 nations. Their doctrine is true and sound and they are calling on people such as Pastor David to re-introduce the fire and power of the Holy Spirit to their people. Their Bishops and leaders are Godly, Spirit-led men, who are providing a platform for Renewal to stretch out its hand, enabling the Pentecostal church and the traditional historical church to both come under the healing power of Christ.

The Vision for Satellite Churches

The satellite churches are an expression of the heart of the central Church, taking the revival message to cities and towns throughout the heart of England. We believe they will increase like spokes in a wheel, fitting securely into the central rim with love and Biblical submission, so that we, as a Church, move together on the roadway of holiness.

The satellite churches function as part of the wider vision of Renewal. All training is given centrally and all of their leaders and Pastors are part of the Renewal wider leadership team. We believe that we will be planting many more Churches throughout the Midlands.

The Ministry of Power Meetings

The Ministry of Power meeting (on a Tuesday evening) came out of a traditional church prayer meeting. Through our desire to see the Holy Spirit move, for Christ to be seen in all of His glory, and Father to be honoured in a way not seen in our nation, the Holy Spirit was invited to take over.

Over the last 4 years the numbers attending have grown, the presence of God has intensified and there have been many miraculous healings testifying of God's grace. We may now need to consider holding Ministry of Power meetings on Wednesday evenings as well as Tuesdays. This meeting is now being taken to 12 cities in the UK.

The Work of Dr Tim Uluirewa

Dr Tim, as many of you may be aware, is a world renowned Worship Director. He gained his doctorate in Music at the London School of Music and is well respected amongst all church traditions. He is now, for the foreseeable future, Director of Worship and Media at Renewal. In this role he oversees the spiritual well being and musical presentation of all of our worship teams. He pastors the Media department and his aim is to bring all of our media and creative ministries into harmony so that they can be seen as a unified ministry bringing glory to God. All forms of music and creative ministry for church and mission are submitted to Dr Tim for consideration and approval.

* *

Partnership

This is what we advise if people want to be part of the fellowship here. We know when you go anywhere new that you are either turned off or turned on, it's simple as that.

You either go, I wouldn't go back there again or oh, this is the greatest thing you've ever seen, brilliant building, fantastic Senior Pastor, which just goes to show how you get wrong impressions when you first come! You get oh, this is God's Church and wonderful. Now what we would do if we were salesmen is say, thank you very much, here's the partnership form sign here and let's have your tithe. But we have learned its God's Church not ours, so what we say to people who join us who are Christians from other Churches, other towns, other countries. We say hey, it's lovely to see you, come join us for at least 3 months. We say, come sit with us for 3 months, get to know us, get to know what we believe, get past the honey moon and see the Senior Pastor's not quite as good looking as you thought he was. That he doesn't always get it right, that the pastors don't always remember your name and sometimes we didn't say hello to you and we have missed your gifting.

Now if after 3 months you think, hey man even with their faults I feel I belong here, then we will speak to you and say, now look you don't have to fully agree with everything we believe other than the absolutes. Tell us about yourself. Now what we do is that if you are joining us from another fellowship - and you can understand this - we would like to contact your previous fellowship. Why would you want to do that? Well, when you move doctor you ask for the records; now you may have left the fellowship and they may through their own reason have been negative about you and it may be just that it was a personality problem and we will listen constructively to all that Church says and we will assess you ourselves and if we feel that perhaps they were insecure themselves once we've taken that on board, we will take that into consideration. So because, a person has joined us from Church B and they have said they are terrible, horrible people we might look at you and say, well it's the insecurity of the Church. But, if you've left that Church and you've not been righteous, we want you to be righteous before you join us because if you join in unrighteousness you bring unrighteousness. Now people do leave this Church. Would you be surprised to know I can't believe why, but they do, because they leave every Church. We say if you join righteous, if you leave, leave righteous. If you leave righteous, you can always come back righteous. If you leave unrighteous, you can't because you generally drift away.

It would be wonderful to be a Pastor of a Church where people only join and never leave, but people leave for all reasons. Somebody offended them, their friends have dropped out with them, they are not doing their job any more and this has happened and that's happened and the next thing you know there is a new Church up the road that's got a brighter sign and a better looking pastor. That's life.

Then we say to you, you've been here 3 months and you've met a pastor who will say, well what do you think? You share that, and we will just give your previous Church a phone or we always give people a letter anyway to take with them.

Maybe you need some help. We have had people say we'd do better in your Church, you are a bigger Church, your more specialised, they are a bit weak in that area. That's fine, that's great, just like a doctor. We don't hold that against you. We've had people join this Church in an absolute mess where most Churches wouldn't touch them, but because we've put discipline in on them and said, now look you realise you were wrong here and you step out of line here you are in real trouble again with us. We will not shower you with gifts if you are under discipline and we feel that's right you are going to stay under discipline, you are going to stay on that course of drugs until you are better.

We are not a soft touch in this Church because we are here to protect you and protect the Church. I am being very faithful to you now. There aren't people just coming here who have got bad habits and bring their bad habits here on our sheep, but we are not here to be lords over you, we are there to help you. If you can take that discipline then we will give it you to bring the best out of you or you will be just on your 6th, 7th, 8th, 9th, 10th Church and spend all your life going round the whirly gig of Churches.

We'd like to think if we are the Church where God wants you to be and why should God send you here and change His mind in a year? God's not double minded so we would like you to think hard before you join us and if you want to join us that's fine, we'll commit ourselves to you and we will endeavour to see God bless you in your life and bring you into your destiny.

So people can come and sit and worship for 3 months, they see a pastor, think that's really good and then we give you a little pack that tells you all again what you've heard before but you can understand and what you do then is just sign a little form that just says, I agree with those things. Why sign a form? Well, it's interesting: you know if we ever have a problem with you over anything rather than it becoming personal, you know, well I don't believe this and I was not told this, we just look up your record and say well we don't want to fall out with you Agnes, you signed to say you believed in the Church's belief in the baptism of the Spirit, you said you believed in water baptism, you've said you have read and understood what we believe, so sweetheart we have not misled you. You signed to say you believed it and that's the end of the argument, because you see we don't want any misunderstanding to come and you see it's good, we sign a driving licence, we sign a passport and we sign our tax and we sign our marriage vows, but some people are frightened to sign to join a Church. They say, well it's unscriptural to sign a form; well I am so glad that I have been signed up in the Lamb's book of life. If Jesus had said that, oh I'm sorry I don't believe in forms. Well He's got one and my name's in there by God's grace and what we do then is on a Sunday we give the right hand of fellowship and make you a partner. We call our members partners because members are something you join, but partners are part of it and Paul said this: **we are partners in the Gospel of Jesus Christ** and so we don't have members, we have partners. We are all in this together as Christ is the Senior Partner. So that is the structure we have.

Thank you for wanting to know more about what the Renewal Christian Centre stands for. We believe God's given us a great vision. He's saying He's going to bring 5,000 people into this place, born again, around the heart of England. We'll be likely opening satellite areas in your area all through Worcestershire and Warwickshire and around parts of Birmingham and all round the areas of Solihull: we are going for it.

So thank you for going through this course and we pray that the days that lie ahead we may be together for the harvest. God bless you and may the Lord be with you all the days of your life.

WEEK 2
WHAT IT MEANS TO BE A CHRISTIAN
WATER BAPTISM

What It Means To Be A Christian

The Power Of The Blood

1 John 1:7   *"But if we walk in the light as He is in the light, we have fellowship with one another, and the blood of Jesus Christ His Son cleanses us from all unrighteousness".*

The blood of Jesus was spilled when He was crucified and if we receive His forgiveness we are saved from sin.

However, what is it about His blood? Many people have shed blood without any affect on our lives.

The blood of Jesus was perfect because it flowed in His body because of His Heavenly Father not His earthly mother. When a foetus is developing in the womb, blood does not pass from mother to baby. So, because of His being conceived by the Holy Spirit, the blood of Jesus is not tainted with sin and is able to cleanse us from all unrighteousness.

When Adam sinned it didn't only affect his descendants - **Romans 3:23 *"For all have sinned and come short of the glory** (standard) **of God".*** (Word in brackets added)

The sin of Adam also brought us under a curse

Genesis 3:17-19   *"Then to Adam He said, 'Because you have heeded the voice of your wife, and have eaten from the tree of which I commanded you, saying, 'You shall not eat of it': 'Cursed is the ground for your sake; in toil you shall eat of it all the days of your life. Both thorns and thistles it shall bring forth for you, and you shall eat the herb of the field. In the sweat of your face you shall eat bread till you return to the ground, for out of it you were taken; for dust you are and* *to dust you shall return¹'"*.

It took the shed blood, death and resurrection of the Lord Jesus Christ to deliver us from that curse.

However,

Galatians 3:13   *"Christ has redeemed us from the curse of the law, having become a curse for us (for it is written, 'Cursed is everyone who hangs on a tree')"*.

Without salvation a curse is upon us from which we cannot break free. Cain found this out to his cost.

Genesis 4:7   *"If you do well, will you not be accepted? And if you do not do well, sin lies at the door. And its desire is for you, but you should rule over it"*.

"Lies at the door" is likened to a crouching lioness preying on her victim waiting for a vulnerable moment.

Christians are able to say no to sin and yes to righteousness because of the blood of Jesus Christ.

The blood of Jesus was spilled and if we receive His forgiveness we are saved from sin.

For the blood of Jesus to cause us to be born again there must be repentance.

What Repentance Really Means

a.   To repent means to turn around, to change, to go in a different direction, to change the way you think.

b.   Repentance is more than being sorry. It is being prepared to change; to go God's way instead of your own way, to do God's will instead of your own.

c.   Without repentance there can be no salvation:

   i.   Acts 2:38 *"Then Peter said to them, 'Repent, and let every one of you be baptised in the name of Jesus Christ for the remission of sins; and you shall receive the gift of the Holy Spirit'"*.

   ii.   Jesus Himself said (Luke 13:3) *"I tell you, no; but unless you repent you will all likewise perish"*.

d. God is full of mercy and patience. However this does not mean we can continue to sin and get away with it. God is not mocked.

  i. ***Hebrews 6:1-8:***

   1 "Therefore, leaving the discussion of the elementary principles of Christ, let us go on to perfection, not laying again the foundation of repentance from dead works and of faith toward God,

   2 of the doctrine of baptisms, of laying on of hands, of resurrection of the dead, and of eternal judgement.

   3 And this we will do if God permits.

   4 For it is impossible for those who were once enlightened, and have tasted the heavenly gift, and have become partakers of the Holy Spirit,

   5 and have tasted the good word of God and the powers of the age to come,

   6 if they fall away, to renew them again to repentance, since they crucify again for themselves the Son of God, and put Him to an open shame.

   7 For the earth which drinks in the rain that often comes upon it, and bears herbs useful for those by whom it is cultivated, receives blessing from God;

   8 but if it bears thorns and briers, it is rejected and near to being cursed, whose end is to be burned".

  ii. God desires all men everywhere to repent:

   2 Peter 3:9 "The Lord is not slack concerning His promise, as some count slackness, but is longsuffering toward us, not willing that any should perish but that all should come to repentance".

  iii. God can never make us repent - it is our choice - He only shows us the way.

What It Means To Be Born Again

Being born again means you are a new creation:

    i. 2 Corinthians 5:17 *"Therefore, if anyone is in Christ, he is a new creation; old things have passed away; behold, all things have become new".*

    ii. A brand new species

        1. Not an improvement on the old through bringing different species together. That does not work in nature. The offspring of two different species are always sterile.

        2. Without a past, only a future.

Adopted

    i. Romans 8:15 *"For you did not receive the spirit of bondage again to fear, but you have received the Spirit of adoption by whom we cry out, Abba, Father".*

    ii. Galatians 4:5 *"To redeem those who were under the law, that we might receive the adoption as sons".*

    iii. Ephesians 1:5 *"Having predestined us to adoption as sons by Jesus Christ to Himself, according to the good pleasure of His will".*

    iv. ADOPTION: The act of taking voluntarily a child of other parents as one's child.

        1. In the New Testament, the Greek word translated adoption literally means, "placing as a son." It is a legal term that expresses the process by which a man brings another person into his family, endowing him with the status and privileges of a biological son or daughter.

        2. In the Old Testament, adoption was never common among the Israelites.

        3. By New Testament times, Roman customs exercised a great deal of influence on Jewish family life. So when Paul used this legal concept of adoption as an analogy to show the believer's relationship to God the people would know exactly what he meant:

            a. The one to be adopted had to be an independent adult

            b. Able to agree to be adopted

            c. Became a New Creature

v. In the eyes of the law the adopted one became:

1. A new creature; he was regarded as being born again into the new family - an illustration of what happens to the believer at conversion

2. Delivered from debt

3. Previous father had no more claim on him

4. It was counted that his previous life never existed

Same Spirit in you as was in Jesus

i. **Romans 8:11-17:**

> **11** *"But if the Spirit of Him that raised up Jesus from the dead dwells in you, He who raised up Christ from the dead will also give life to your mortal bodies through His Spirit who dwells in you.*
>
> **12** *Therefore, brethren, we are debtors - not to the flesh, to live after the flesh.*
>
> **13** *For if you live according the flesh, you will die: but if by the Spirit you put to death the deeds of the body, you will live.*
>
> **14** *For as many as are led by the Spirit of God, these are sons of God.*
>
> **15** *For you did not receive the spirit of bondage again to fear, but you received the Spirit of adoption by whom we cry out, Abba, Father.*
>
> **16** *The Spirit Himself bears witness with our spirit that we are the children of God,*
>
> **17** *And if children, then heirs - heirs of God and joint heirs with Christ, if indeed we suffer with Him, that we may also be glorified together".*

ii. "The presence of the Spirit of God in believers guarantees that the God who raised up Christ from the dead will quicken the mortal bodies of believers through His Spirit dwelling in (them). A mortal body is a body capable of dying. A body made alive by the Holy Spirit becomes immortal. The transition from mortality to immortality is the work of the Spirit" (from Wycliffe Commentary).

iii. If you are a joint heir then everything one receives the other also receives. So we are able to affirm that all that the Father has for His Son the Lord Jesus Christ, He has also for us, His sons.

Water Baptism

Water baptism is a very fundamental step in the Christian life

1. What Leads Us To Think About Baptism?

- a. **Acts 2:37**

    Before this verse Peter has been preaching to the Jews about Jesus and about themselves.

    Then in **verse 37** we read, *"Now when they heard this, they were cut to the heart, and said to Peter and the rest of the apostles, 'Men and brethren, what shall we do?' "*.

    They were convicted. They realised they were sinners and separated from God and needed to do something about it.

- b. Peter confronted the people with four things:

    1. That Jesus is the Son of God who died on the Cross.

    2. That we are by nature selfish creatures that want to go our own way, and have no time for God.

    3. That God created us and wants us to be united with Him so that life can have meaning.

    4. Jesus died so that we can find our way back to God, have our sins forgiven, and receive the life of God.

- c. This is the starting point of baptism:

    1. To recognise that God loves us.

    2. To admit that we are sinners.

    3. To receive God's forgiveness

    4. To repent and be baptised.

    Repent means to change direction from living for self - the way of the world and its standards - and to turn and go God's way.

2. **When To Be Baptised**

   a. Mark 16:16 *"He who believes and has been baptised will be saved".*

   b. Acts 8:12 *"But when they believed Philip as he preached he things concerning the kingdom of God and the name of Jesus Christ, both men and women were baptised".*

   c. Acts 18:8 *"Then Crispus, the ruler of the synagogue, believed on the Lord with all his household. And many of the Corinthians, hearing, believed and were baptised".*

       i. Baptism always follows belief in Jesus. After John the Baptist there is no instance in the Bible of someone receiving baptism without believing in who Jesus is, what He has done, and repentance.

       ii. It is not a "fluffy, magical moment" but a definite act and step of obedience we need to take.

3. **What Baptism Means**

   a. Baptise = Baptizo (bap-tid'-zo) (Greek: dye of a cloth) = to immerse.

   "It is used in the New Testament in Luke 11:38 of washing oneself (as in 2 Kings 5:14, "dipped himself'); see also Isaiah 21:4, lit. "lawlessness overwhelms me." In the early chapters of the four Gospels and in Acts 1:5; 11:16; 19:4, it is used of the rite performed by John the Baptist who called upon the people to repent "confessing their sins", thus acknowledging their unfitness to be in the Messiah's coming kingdom. Distinct from this is the "baptism" enjoined by Christ, Matthew 28:19, a "baptism" to be undergone by believers, thus witnessing to their identification with Him in death, burial and resurrection, e.g., Acts 19:5; Romans 6:3-4; 1 Corinthians 1:13-17; 12:13; Galatians 3:27; Colossians 2:12. The phrase in Matthew 28:19, "baptising them into the Name" (RV; cf. Acts 8:16, RV), would indicate that the "baptised" person was closely bound to, or became the property of the one whose name he was "baptised"" (from Vine's Expository Dictionary of Biblical Words).

   b. In baptism we are following Jesus.

       i. In all four gospels you will find an account of the baptism of Jesus.

   c. Baptism is a commandment of Jesus.

Matthew 28:19   *"Go therefore and make disciples of all the nations, baptising them in the name of Father and of the Son and of the Holy Spirit".*

    d.   We are identifying with the death, burial, and resurrection of Jesus.

         i. Going down in the water we are identifying with the death of Jesus. A putting to death of our old life and all it stands for *(Romans 6:4).*

         ii. While under the water we are identifying with the burial of Jesus. A burial of the old sinful life and nature *(Colossians 3:8-10).*

         iii. Coming up out of the water we are identifying with the resurrection of Jesus. A declaration that we are going to live for Jesus as His disciple *(Romans 6:9-13).*

4. After Baptism: What Then?

Acts 2:42   *"And they continued steadfastly in the apostles' doctrine and fellowship, in the breaking of bread, and in prayers".*

1. Baptism is not a magical formula. If you don't feed a baby it will grow very weak. If we don't feed our spiritual lives they too will become very weak.

2. Teaching is the ministry of the Word of God. We must build ourselves up in the Word of God, not wait for trials and temptations. Greek word for God's Word is "sperma". God's word is His very life and seed. The enemy has no defence against it. Hallelujah! Remember Jesus in the wilderness. What was His defence? Word of God every time *(Matthew 4:4).* This is a most powerful weapon and must not be ignored.

3. Fellowship will help maintain the glow of your Christian life.

4. Breaking of bread (Communion). "Do this in remembrance of Me" said Jesus. So Communion is a commandment.

5. Prayer. Personal prayer and corporate prayer are very important. This is vital in our lives.

In the New Testament every time someone believed in Jesus they were baptised. Baptism doesn't mean we will not have any problems after we are baptised.

It means we are no longer Satan's territory but living in the Kingdom of God with direct access to God for help in time of trouble.

WEEK 3
INTRODUCTION TO CELLS

Welcome and Overview

The most effective way of caring for and nurturing people in a church environment is by meeting in small groups. This is evidenced in part by the effectiveness of courses such as Alpha where the small group plays an integral part of the evening; and if run properly is a very effective evangelistic tool.

We are going to be looking tonight at a brief history of cell church, what constitutes a cell (dynamics), the Renewal Christian Centre cell model and how you can become part of the pastoral care/cell ministry here.

Why Cell Church?

Four reasons why cell church is a popular way of caring for the church population:

1. Unworkable care structures.

No matter how hard we try, it becomes impossible to really care, relate and minister to an ever-increasingly large group of people personally and effectively. You cannot keep on taking on more and more full and part-time staff - this is not an effective use of the body of Christ. Besides which the body gets bored or lazy when they are not being used!

Take the analogy of the football pitch - 11 people desperately in need of a rest with 11,000 needing some exercise!

2. An increasing inability to release believers into effective ministry.

Because our structure suggests that the main time and location for ministry is 'Sunday Church' only a handful can effectively be involved, leaving masses of untapped potential in the body.

There is a real danger in seeing the Pastor/Leader as the only one who can do church.

3. Evangelistic ineffectiveness, especially considering the potential of such a large group of believers.

With all that we do, all that we are and all that we organise, most believers have very little meaningful contact with non-Christians and the vast majority will not lead one person to Christ this year and almost all the growth, even in large churches is going to be transfer growth.

Look at what Jesus did with just 12 apostles... They didn't hoard all of the work to themselves, they went out and began to fulfil the Great Commission.

4. An inability to provide an effective forum for application and accountability to the Word of God taught in the large group celebration.

In other words believers come week by week and sit under the Word, but how do we know that people are changing their behaviour?

The following questions need to be addressed if we are to experience radical growth:

How can a growing church mobilise the members into effective ministry?

How can we go further in our care for one another, making sure that every committed member of the body feels secure in the knowledge that help is on hand if needed?

When will we have the time to do all these things in an ever increasingly busy social climate?

How can we create a forum for the application of the Sunday teaching?

Are we doing good things at the expense of the best?

How can we encourage one another to be bold in talking to people about Jesus?

How can we facilitate relationships that are real where those with deep needs can be ministered to?

How can we effectively introduce our neighbours to the reality of Christ's love for them?

How can we effectively disciple new converts and bring them through to maturity in Christ?

I believe the answer lies in understanding that small groups (cell groups) are just as important as a large group celebration.

There are four perspectives that will outline why the church needs to take hold of cell principles and run with them - this list is not exclusive, however it does give us a good start!

1. Biblical Perspective

The Jethro principle:

Exodus 18:13-26 - READ ALL

"And they continued steadfastly in the apostles' doctrine and fellowship, in the breaking of bread, and in prayers". Acts 2:42

"So continuing daily with one accord in the temple, and breaking bread from house to house, they ate their food with gladness and simplicity of heart, praising God and having favour with all the people. And the Lord added to the church daily those who were being saved". Acts 2:46-47

"And He Himself gave some to be apostles, some prophets, some evangelists, and some pastors and teachers, for the equipping of the saints for the work of the ministry, for the edifying of the body of Christ, till we all come to the unity of the faith and of the knowledge of the Son of God, to a perfect man, to the measure of the stature of the fullness of Christ". Ephesians 4:11-13

Firstly, let's look at what we can learn from the Church of the New Testament, the first Church.

Acts 2:42 *"And they continued steadfastly in the apostles' doctrine and fellowship, in the breaking of bread, and in prayers.*

43 *Then fear came upon every soul, and many wonders and signs were done through the apostles.*

44 *Now all who believed were together, and had all things in common,*

45 *And sold their possession and goods, and divided them among all, as anyone had need.*

46 *So continuing daily with one accord in the temple, and breaking bread from house to house, they ate their food with gladness and simplicity of heart,*

47 *Praising God and having favour with all the people. And the Lord added to the Church daily those who were being saved".*

Six verses of Scripture, describing a kind of church lifestyle that was to continue for almost a quarter of a millennium and a model of Christianity that almost won the World.

The only thing that seemed to change was the frequency that they met!

2. Wesleyan Perspective

Below are some of the concepts that form the bulwark of John Wesley's educational philosophy:

- Learning comes by doing the will of God.

- Mankind's nature is perfected by participation in groups, not by acting as isolated individuals.

- The spirit and the practice of primitive Christianity can and must be recaptured.

- The primary function of spiritual/educational leadership is to equip others to lead and minister, not to perform the ministry personally.

Commentators on Methodism state:

"Every Methodist was under someone else's direct and immediate supervision. There was a constant emphasis on 'bearing one another's burdens,' so that not even the slightest affliction went unnoticed".

"Each instructional grouping within the Wesleyan system was related to the ones above and below it in the hierarchy…The leading members of one group were almost always participants in the next group up the ladder".

The revival that began with Whitfield as the leader, later became known as "The Wesleyan Revival." This was because Wesley did not just preach to the masses. Wesley followed the example of Jesus and focussed on equipping people to disciple one another. Wesley developed a discipling process that he used successfully for forty years. Even though he never drew as many people as Whitfield, at his death he left behind a movement. George Whitfield said:

"My brother Wesley acted wisely…the souls that were awakened under his ministry, he joined in a class, and thus preserved the fruits of his labour. This I neglected, and my people are a rope of sand".

Wesley, like Jesus, focussed on developing and implementing a process that enabled disciples to grow, who then developed and supported other disciples.

3. The Free Methodist Perspective

"If the local church becomes known for its discipling ministry, Free Methodism will grow strong. If not, the church will be seriously weakened by a generation of members stunted in their spiritual growth". A Future with a History - the Wesleyan Witness of the Free Methodist Church by David L. McKenna.

"Within the church, we should regularly see reproduction of disciples, leaders, cells and churches. Disciples produce disciples; leaders produce leaders; cells produce cells; and churches produce churches. To assume that only evangelists and teachers produce disciples, and conferences plant churches, is to miss the power and the reproductive nature of the body of Christ - to say nothing of missing the joy of personally participating in Kingdom expansion". Every Local Church a Reproducing Congregation by Bishop Kevin L. Mannoia (North American Bishop).

4. Jesus' Perspective

Jesus, who had compassion for the multitudes, left the crowds for the sake of His twelve, for the sake of the crowds.

"And this gospel of the kingdom will be preached in all the world as a witness to all the nations, and then the end will come" Matthew 24:14.

What is a cell?

Ask any medical student "What is a cell?" and they will explain that it is the basic building block of the body.

Our bodies consist of millions and millions of cells working in unison. We cannot live without them. Within each cell is carried the DNA, the genetic coding, or "blueprint" of life itself. Through our bodies we can reach out and touch the world around us. Otherwise we would be disembodied spirits, unable to influence and impact our world. By nature cells will seek to multiply themselves, reproducing after their own kind, or transitioning to fulfil different functions according to hormonal influences. What is true of the physical body is true of the body of Christ, the Church. After all, truth is parallel.

Spiritual DNA

We see the origins of the church began with Jesus calling 'the twelve' to Him. His 'Master plan' was to create a small intimate fellowship of disciples around Him, pouring His life - His 'DNA' - into them. It was in this small "cell" gathering that Jesus built relationship with them, taught and trained them, imparted authority and power, and sent them out to minister and witness.

"Then He appointed twelve, that they might be with Him and that He might send them out to preach and to have power to heal sicknesses and cast out demons" (Mark 3:14-15).

Later, the Holy Spirit would reproduce the same kind of ministry in the lives of subsequent believers.

After Pentecost, we see the life and vigour of the Early Church maintained by their large, corporate gatherings in the Temple, complemented with their much smaller fellowship meetings in believers' homes *(Acts 2:41 - 47)*.

The Apostles Had A Cell Vision

A vital church grows in Jerusalem. It is a church endued with supernatural power *(Acts 2:43)*. The DNA of Jesus has been successfully reproduced from Christ's 'twelve' to this burgeoning new church in Acts *(Acts 4:13)*. They know how to construct their lives upon the Word of God. They know how to create close fellowship with each other so that no one is in need. They know how to reach out in revival power to the lost, restoring damaged lives. They know how to draw the attention of both God and Man *(Acts 2:47)*. Integral to the Holy Spirit finding a welcome place in the life of the early church was the place of the 'cell' gatherings.

After the destruction of the Jerusalem Temple, the Church grew rapidly and spread throughout the entire known world at that time. They erected no church buildings of their own. How, then, did they achieve such explosive growth? They continued to meet in each other's homes as "cells".

Throughout the history of the Church, whenever the Holy Spirit needed to move in revival power, the phenomena of cells was used as the structure to convey His restorative works. A prime example is the ministry of John Wesley and his 'classes' for believers. In more recent history, over the last thirty years, we see those churches throughout the world that are experiencing explosive growth are Cell Churches.

The Beginning

The focus of Jesus' teaching was 'kingdom' not 'church'. The Kingdom means the rule and reign of God. Jesus' ministry was to preach the gospel, heal the sick, cast out demons, feed the hungry and reprove those who oppressed the poor and He trained His disciples to carry on and extend His ministry.

The Church (or the community of the King) is to carry on the ministry of Jesus. Our job is to advance the rule and reign of God by destroying Satan's work *(Matthew 10:7-8; 16:17-20; 18:18-20; Luke 10:18-20; John 14:12)*.

The Church is the agent of the kingdom, moving upon the earth - it is a counter culture - a new social reality - called to fulfil the three tasks God has given to mankind at the beginning:

1) Carry the image of God;

2) Spread the presence of God - multiplication;

3) Exercise the authority of God - subdue, have dominion.

(Read Genesis 1:26-28).

The early church lived in an atmosphere of prophecy, revelation, signs, wonders and miracles. The Book of Acts is a thirty-year record of the power of the Holy Spirit supernaturally extending the kingdom of God and building the Church, through both apostles and people.

One day Jesus will return to bring in His kingdom fully - for now it is spiritual, a mystery, hidden **(Matthew 13:1; Mark 4:11; Luke 8:10; 17:20-21).** Then it will be revealed, physical and visible and will be over all the earth **(Daniel 7:13-14; Isaiah 9:6-7; Revelation 11:15; 1 Corinthians 15:24-28; 2 Timothy 4:1).**

The kingdom is prophesied in the OT, taught in the NT and seen in the Book of Revelation. As the Church Age draws to a close and the Kingdom Age draws nearer we should expect increasing revelation **(Daniel 12:4a, 9).**

The goal of the kingdom is to sum up all things in Christ and establish God's reign over all His creation **(Colossians 1:20).** All of history is moving unstoppably in this direction.

Pentecost was the birthday of the church. The Holy Spirit came on the 120 believers gathered in the upper room **(Acts 2:1-4).** Peter, now filled with the Holy Spirit, preaches a sermon to the crowds - **Acts 2:41 "Then those who gladly received his word were baptised; and that day three thousand souls were added to them".**

Soon after, Peter preached again (**Acts 4:4**) **"...many of those who heard the word believed; and the number of men came to be about five thousand".** So in a few weeks there are at least 8,000 new believers in Jerusalem and from all over - what happened to them? Where did they meet and what did they do when they did meet?

Acts 2:46 *"So continuing daily with one accord in the temple, and breaking bread from house to house, they ate their food with gladness and simplicity of heart".*

They met in two places - the temple for those in Jerusalem (or the public place, which was available to them at that time) and in homes (where they lived).

Acts 2:42 *"And they continued steadfastly in the apostles' doctrine and fellowship, in the breaking of bread, and in prayers".*

Acts 2:47 *"Praising God and having favour with all the people. And the Lord added to the church daily those who were being saved".*

History has moved the modern Church a long way from the Church that God founded by the Holy Spirit in the years following Pentecost.

The early Church did not meet primarily or essentially for corporate worship, evangelism, listening to a sermon or even for fellowship! However, they did do these things...

The 1st Century Church did meet for mutual edification

1 Corinthians 14:26 Order in Church Meetings

"How is it then, brethren? Whenever you come together, each of you has a psalm, has a teaching, has a tongue, has a revelation, has an interpretation. Let all things be done for edification".

Ephesians 5:18-21

> 18 *"And do not be drunk with wine, in which is dissipation; but be filled with the Spirit,*
>
> 19 *speaking to one another in psalms and hymns and spiritual songs, singing and making melody in your heart to the Lord,*
>
> 20 *giving thanks always for all things to God the Father in the Name of our Lord Jesus Christ,*
>
> 21 *submitting to one another in the fear of God".*

Everyone was able to participate in building up and encouraging one another. There was no worship team **(Ephesians 5:19; Colossians 3:16)** and no preacher for the day **(Ephesians 4:16)**. It was a meeting where believers exercised freshness, openness, spontaneity and accountability with every member involved - face-to-face.

Evangelism took place where unbelievers met - often synagogues and market places **(Acts 14:1; 17:1-33; 18:4,19)**.

Apostles did bring the Word of God at special large meetings (the Sunday services and conferences of the day) - **(Acts 5:40-42; 19:9-10; 20:27,31)**.

The Church met in the homes of its members for the first 300 years after Pentecost. There are some seventeen references in the NT of believers meeting in simple, ordinary homes **(Acts 2:2, 46; 8:3; 9:11; 10:32; 12:12; 16:15, 34, 40; 17:5; 18:7; 20:20; 21:8; Romans 16:3-5; 1 Corinthians 16:19; Colossians 4:15; Philippians 2; 2 John 10)**.

As the numbers grew so more and more homes were involved.

3 Observations:

1) People are God's house;

It is the saints who are called the house of God (living stones), never the building.

It is the believers indwelt with God's life who are named the Church.

2) The home is best suited for:

Mutual participation

The exercise of spiritual gifts

The building together of community

The communal need

Open transparency and mutual submission

Freedom of dialogue

Shared life in the Spirit

The purpose of God in building the body together into the Head, Christ; the Body of Christ will become the bride of Christ - not many brides, only one.

The Apostles, in their letters, give 58 references to 'one another', each one an exhortation to harmonious living.

3. The home reflects a simple family atmosphere:

It encourages humility (no place for pride to show!).

It has no extra overhead costs (money was freed for apostolic Church planting and feeding the poor and widows).

Everyone can be known, accepted and encouraged - neither can people hide sin in their lives…

There is no opportunity for the growth of a spectator mentality.

You can be yourself and find relevance, reality and authenticity.

Cell Dynamics

***Ephesians 4:16**   "From Him the whole body joined and held together by every supporting ligament grows and builds itself up in love as each part does it's work".*

There are seven verbs in verse 16 and these summarise how the body of Christ should function smoothly and they are as follows: -

Joining

Holding

Supporting

Growing

Building

Loving

Working

We are going to take a look at each of these principles in order.

JOINING

In some ways the secular world in terms of sports clubs organisations have a similarity to the way that the Church operates in that there is a distinction between members and non-members.

Again different denominations have different procedures for acceptance into membership. The Anglican Church, for example, has a confirmation service, confirmation classes and baptism symbolising entry into the worldwide communion rather than into membership into a particular parish. In Baptist Churches there would be an interview with a couple of the Deacons and a vote at full church meeting.

Many Churches of all styles have commitment classes or commitment courses ranging from a few weeks to a few months and there is a great merit in this approach because a course offers a new person the opportunity to understand what membership means and this particular local expression of Church. New members to the Church need to understand the responsibility and the vision for cells and their respective role in this cell group and what is expected of them.

HOLDING

The NIV uses the phrase 'holding', other versions use 'knitting together' and it's very graphic and describes an integration that we should be aiming towards.

Finding and keeping new people is not easy. We can tell by the response cards that we get that a lot a lot of people raise their hands and walk to the front, especially at rallies. However, we are not talking about responses, but about people who come regularly, who are discipled and stay with us.

We need to consider the people who have made a degree of commitment not only to God, but also to the local Church setting and their cell group. The initial experience is that of being a babe in Christ and it's a wonderful time for them, they are the focus of attention. They get top quality milk and they have their nappies changed for them, spiritually of course. There is a fresh person joining and therefore the group dynamic changes, but it is an important time for the cell to go through this phase and to check the Christian status of the whole group.

SUPPORTING

Support is a two-way thing, group leaders will regularly be asked to give support to others, but it's necessary that the leader also has support. With the cascade type of cell leadership, which we will learn about later on, the cell leader is himself in a cell and also has his own cell to run and so therefore there are two cell meetings a week. Therefore for example, Pastor David has two cells of leaders that include the Pastors, Elders and Trustees. I am in Pastor David's cell and I also have a cell of my own. Some of my men are also running cells.

I am going to put a diagram up on the OHP, which looks at support in more detail, and this is how we can offer a certain amount of support to our group.

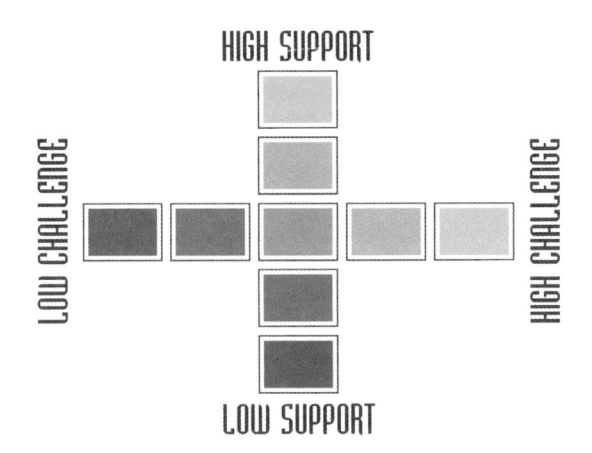

HIGH SUPPORT

LOW CHALLENGE **HIGH CHALLENGE**

LOW SUPPORT

There are four possible scenarios to the matrix of support and challenge and our goal is for people to be experiencing high challenge with the appropriate level of support. The worst option is the bottom left, which shows low challenge and low support; as the old adage goes, there's a lot of apathy around but then nobody seems to care.

The challenge is for cell leaders to attain a level of excitement, growth and fulfilment within the group without isolating people or smothering people as in the other two corners.

GROWING

It is clear from Scripture that God wants us to grow and move on and to grow in the fruit and the gifts of the Holy Spirit. It is also true to say that not everybody recognises the need for growth. A lot of people don't like change and therefore the challenge of growing can be different for different people. We have to look at ways to challenge members and to grow members. Opportunities to grow could be similar to the following: - Opportunities in any form of ministry, be it beyond their proven ability, being careful obviously, discussing with people how they hope to develop, the expression of their gifts and handling mistakes in a positive and encouraging way.

BUILDING

Building is interesting in as much as I might grow if I was stranded on a desert island. My prayer life might get more attention, I might become a real expert on the various vegetation and the berries that are out there, especially those that can cause short-term damage, but I would not be able to build. The dimension of building needs other people to interact with who will grind up my rough edges as iron sharpens up iron - I can't be a Christian alone. That is not how God made us; it's not good for man to be alone.

Another facet of building in the small group is linked to synergy, the point being the group can be better than the sum of it's parts, i.e. two plus two can make five. The cell group dynamic means I need you although I might not always find you comfortable.

The verse that we are looking at here, **Ephesians 4:16,** doesn't just talk about building but it talks about the body building itself up and it's a spiritual phenomenon. Unfortunately many teams, groups and organisations do the opposite, they knock themselves down. Groups take a certain amount of energy just to stand still, dealing with things like administration, pastoral needs and issues.

The ability of a group to build itself up is the spiritual energy and synergy that means nobody need be exhausted by striving to make it happen, that everyone gives a little and is more effective in the kingdom of God. So, examples of groups building up could include social activities together, learning to appreciate the complimentary ways of thinking and having some fun together.

LOVING

I could keep you here for weeks talking about love as God is love but we do need to be aware, based on **1 Corinthians 13 *"that love is patient and kind, it doesn't envy, it doesn't parade itself, it does not behave rudely, it doesn't seek it's own, it's not provoked and it thinks no evil. It bears all things, believes all things and hopes all things".*** So tremendous, that's the challenge of cell.

Some examples of loving might include acts of kindness, affirmation of the person in terms of vocal affirmation, remembering things like birthdays or when someone is going through an issue or a problem in their life that you stick by them rather than let them get on with it on their own.

WORKING

It's much better at looking at working together after the first six points because now you are at a sense of relationship that you can work together more effectively and you will understand more about how you can work together. The working is definitely evangelistic, it's out-looking, it's working on outreach and inviting non-Christian friends, family, friends or neighbours to maybe a barbecue or a bowling evening or whatever.

Maybe on to an Alpha course for example and through these seven points we will see that the small group, the cell, provides the minimum structure for the first level of pastoral care.

The Renewal Christian Centre Cell Model

"The things you have heard me say. . entrust to reliable men. . who will also teach others". (Paul to Timothy, **2 Timothy 2:2**)

Pastor David will lead two men's cells, and Molly Carr will lead one women's cell, each group to contain 12 people. Each member of these groups will themselves have a group of between 7 and 12 people as their cell. They will impart shepherding principles and practices to their cells.

Partners will be encouraged to join cells. As partners receive training in the cells, they may be encouraged to go on the 'cell leadership' course. Gradually cell principles will be incorporated into the whole church.

Cells meet for only 1 hour per week, at any time of the day or night convenient to the members of that cell, plus any travelling time.

The idea of 'cascading' is that training starts at the top of an organisation. It begins with the leaders and managers. These leaders take ownership of what they have been taught, assimilate it, put it into practice and subsequently train the groups that they serve. Members of the group then have the responsibility for 'cascading' the knowledge to others in the same way.

How does the 'Cascade Principle' work in practice?

The calling is to find twelve and to reproduce Christ's character in them so that they can each reproduce Christ's character in others. In our case Pastor David (men) and Molly (women) will disciple leaders in cells of twelve, as Jesus did.

These leaders act as envoys or diplomats, each of them discipling cells of between seven and twelve in the teaching and vision they have received. They are accountable for maintaining the purity and integrity of the vision, values and lifestyle. The members of these cells become leaders (shepherds) of other cells, and so on.

The idea is that everyone is to progress to being in two cells, one as a cell member, and one as a cell leader. There is no dividing of cells. A cell is an 'open cell' until it is full i.e. leader + 7-12.

Example of Cascade Leadership:

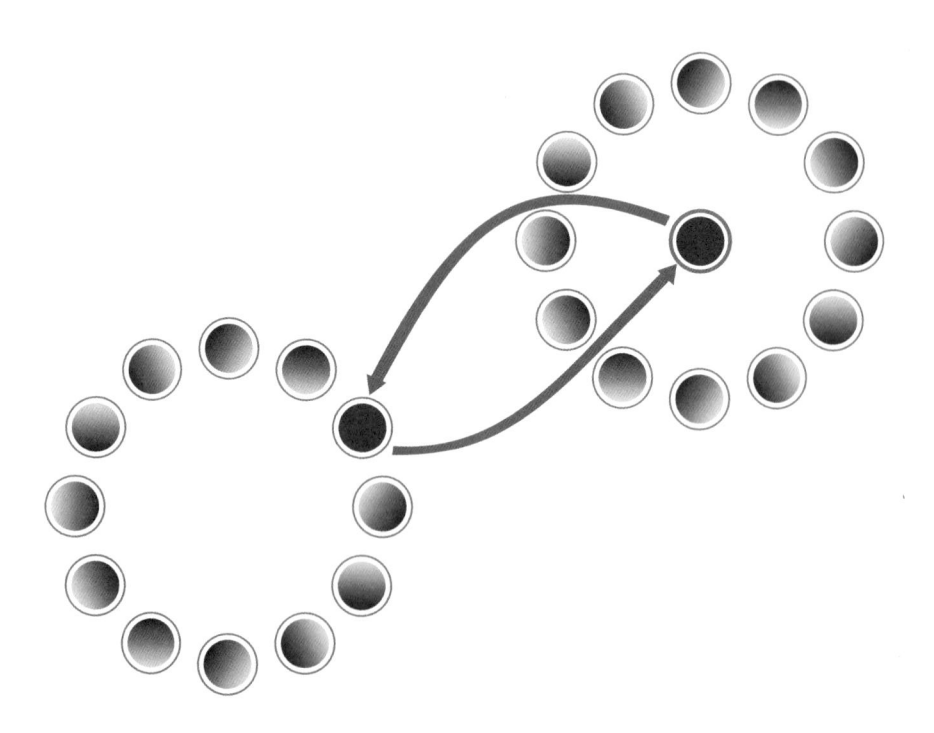

Three keys for successful cell group integration

Key One

The groups are homogenous i.e. there are men's cells and women's cells and youth cells. Cells for children are mixed (male and female). There may be some adult mixed sex cells e.g. in the short term when numbers are low in the pioneer areas (Satellites), or cells specifically for older people. There may be a few couple's cells e.g. for helping marriages.

Homogenous cells allow people to grow with others that are like-minded and face the same challenges, have the same sorts of needs, share similar interest, identity and language. This means that all ministries within the church are run along cell principles.

There are three facts that will help us to grasp the importance of homogenous groups:

1. The church is a family.
2. Each member has special interest, needs and concerns.
3. Each group is best equipped to reach and disciple others like themselves.

This means that men are best equipped to reach and disciple men, women best to reach and disciple women, and so on.

Key Two

We are still one body and meet together for corporate worship. A family must regularly come together as a family, but there will be times when the children are doing one thing, the teens are doing something else and the father and mother are engaged in yet other activities. The family is where we should first be discipled, then move into homogenous cells.

Key Three

Discipleship is about role models and teaching by example. A man cannot model for a woman how to be a good wife, neither can a woman model for a man how to be the husband who loves his wife as Christ loves the Church.

How do we use the hour in a cell meeting?

"And they continued steadfastly in the apostles' doctrine and fellowship, in the breaking of bread and in prayers" Acts 2:42.

This Scripture is the model we aim to follow. We are devoted to the Word of God and to prayer. We share with each other in the breaking of bread and in fellowship. We are friends and care for one another first, then we focus on becoming friends with our neighbours and the people we meet in the street, and in our daily work, so that they can discover the immediacy of God's love, through us.

We plan for and embrace 4 W's:

Welcome - share blessings and needs.

Walk (life) - give thanks for the blessings and pray for the needs. Bring comfort and perhaps counsel.

Word - discuss Renewal's vision, and the current preached/prophetic Word, emphasising experience and action.

It is not intended that cell leaders will have to prepare material to teach. Rather they should keep themselves prepared. Morning sermon notes covering the general theme will be available from time to time.

Witness - pray over a list of the non-Christians. Discuss ways of making and developing relationships.

The underlying premise of each session is that we know how to experience the growth of the Word in our lives, so that we sow seed and reap a harvest. It is about practical Christian living.

Cell Leader Training

There will be several different methods of cell leadership training with the RBTC being the umbrella for any training.

Finally -

How Do I Become Part Of The Cell Ministry At Renewal Christian Centre?

The Community Pastor holds a database of all cells that are operating within the church, the database includes the name of the cell leader, where the cell meets and when (day and time) and also who is part of the cell.

Cells are built primarily on relationships, then geography. Therefore cell leaders (as Jesus did) should ask those that they feel the Lord is impressing on them to follow them (i.e. become part of their cell group).

If you have a friendship with someone already in a cell, ask whether you can join his or her cell (relationship). If they have a vacancy, you will be introduced to the cell leader and if suitable then you will be allowed to take part as a guest in the first instance. If everything works out then you will become a full member, otherwise you will have the option of finding another group.

If you do not know anyone in a cell yet, then please leave your name and contact details at the Information Desk for the attention of the Community Pastor. He will then endeavour to introduce you to a cell leader meeting reasonably close to your home address (geography).

I trust that you have been inspired by this teaching on cell church and the potential of Christians living in community, nurturing one another and winning friends and family to Christ.

WEEK 4
FINANCE, GIVING & STEWARDSHIP

Tithing

First, some facts:

o   The term "to tithe", or "tithing", is a Biblical one.

o   It is mentioned approximately 38 times throughout the O.T.& N.T.

o   Technically, it means giving a tenth of all we receive back to God. Why? Because according to **Leviticus 27 v 30 ff**. IT BELONGS TO HIM! - **"A tithe of everything from the land, whether grain from the soil or fruit from the trees, BELONGS TO THE LORD ....The ENTIRE TITHE of the herd and flock will be holy to the Lord ".** (Capitals added)

o   Tithing is far more than a legal requirement (despite the fact that the tithe belongs to the Lord!). In **Genesis 14 v 18-20** (long before the stating of God's Law to Moses) we discover it's *already in the heart of Abram!*

o   Through his action, Abram recognised a "Divineness" or "God-ness" about Melchizedek and acknowledged it by his tithe to him! (Also note, Jacob promised to tithe to God - **Genesis 28 v22** - again, recognition that the One he worshipped was God).

o   Therefore, for us also, recognition of the Lord Jesus as our God should be acknowledged by our tithe to Him.

o   So, tithing is not only an act of obedience, but it's also an *acknowledgement of the Lord Jesus as our God.*

o   **No tithe - no acknowledgement!**

o   Our tithe should be unlimited.

Matthew 10 v 8   *"Freely you have received, freely give".*

Luke 12 v 48   *"Everyone who has been given much, much will be demanded".*

o   We've moved from the limitation of the law (10% tithe) to the extravagance of grace! i.e. - **Unlimited giving!**

- It's really a matter of the heart, not so much the actual amount, e.g. **Exodus 25 v 1&2**- Israelites who "had a heart to give."

Mark 12 v 41-44 -the widow's offering.

- New Testament affirms tithing!

- Jesus Himself affirms tithing is right to do, but only in the context of a righteous, faithful life - **Matthew 23 v 23.**

- Withholding our tithe robs God and deprives us of great blessing - **Malachi 3 v 8-12.**

- Because tithing is a matter of the heart, to withhold our tithe is to withhold our heart from God.

- Tithing activates a spiritual law or principle.

- What do laws/principles do? They **determine the course of action of things or people!** e.g. the Law of Gravity pulls objects/us **down,** but the Law of Aerodynamics **overcomes it and lifts things up!**

- Our hoarding and greed is like the Law of Gravity. Our tithing and generosity is like the Law of Aerodynamics - the one keeps us earthbound in poverty and need; the other lifts us high into the supernatural, superabundance of God's provision!

- Read **Proverbs 3 v 9 & 10, and 2 Corinthians 9 v 6.**

- The tithe supports the Church's ministry.

- In the O.T. tithes supported the priestly ministry - **Numbers 18 v 21.** Today, they're to support God's work in churches and missions. Therefore, tithes are vital to its ongoing.

- Remember - tithe into "good soil "i.e. Bible-based, Spirit filled, authoritative church.

- Tithe accurately!

Malachi 3 v 10   *"Bring the whole tithe into the storehouse . ….."*.

- i.e. tithe from your **gross** income.

- Tithe cheerfully!

2 Corinthians 9 v 7.

Stewardship

The Christian, according to the Bible, is a BRAND NEW CREATION!

"Therefore, if anyone is in Christ, he is a new creation; old things have passed away; behold, all things have become new" **(2 Corinthians 5 v 17).**

That "brand new creation" came at huge expense - the life of the Son of God.

For most of us, a brand new expensive purchase gets treated very carefully, **especially if it's not ours, but on loan!**

According to the Bible, that is exactly what our lives are - EXPENSIVE PURCHASES THAT ARE NOT OUR OWN, BUT ON LOAN! Listen to what the Bible says:

"Or do you not know that your body is the temple of the Holy Spirit, who is in you, whom you have from God, and you are NOT YOUR OWN? For YOU WERE BOUGHT AT A PRICE…." **(1 Corinthians 6 v 19&20)** *(Capitals added).*

So, who we are and **what** we have, is **not our own - it's God's!** Our job is to be CAREFUL STEWARDS of it.

What then, is a Steward?

- someone with a delegated responsibility.

- someone entrusted to direct or control the use of another's property or power e.g. Adam in the Garden of Eden.

Today, God has given His Church a responsibility: He has entrusted us to direct or control His property and His power!

To illustrate this and understand the seriousness of it, look at **Matthew 25 v14-30** (Message Bible) noting especially ***v28-30: "Take the thousand and give it to the one who risked the most. And get rid of this "play-it-safe" who won't go out on a limb. Throw him out into utter darkness".***

What's it saying?

- supernaturally successful, seriously radical stewardship is called for!

Notice from the passage:

- o Who are the "stewards?"***(v.14)*** - His **servants** (i.e. **believers**).

- o What were they given? ***(v. 15) - responsibility*** according to **ability.**

- o Why is "good stewardship" so important? Because God has made us

STEWARDS OF ETERNAL LIFE.

This "eternal life" (i.e. God-centred life) impacts on our:

- o   Relationship with God.
- o   Relationship with others.
- o   Successes.
- o   Failures.
- o   Emotions.
- o   Marriages.
- o   Parenting.
- o   Businesses.
- o   Finances.
- o   Abilities.
- o   Ministries.

What we do with this ETERNAL LIFE - how well we "steward" it will determine our ETERNAL DESTINY: **Matthew 25 v 20-30.**

God's saying: RISK TAKERS REQUIRED!

No place in the Kingdom of God for "play-it-safe" Christians who won't "go out on a limb!"

e.g. Jonathan (He & armour-bearer against Philistines - *1 Samuel 14 v 1-15*) & David (vs. Goliath - 1 *Samuel 17*) - "risk takers" for God!

Matthew 11v12   *"And from the days of John the Baptist until now the kingdom of heaven suffers violence, and the violent take it by force".*

Regardless of size of responsibility, *if handled well*, will result in **EQUALLY GREAT REWARD.** The one given 5 talents who made 5 more, and the one given 2 who made 2 more, both became "partners" with God! *Matthew 25 v 20-23.*

Financial Stewardship

How do finances achieve God's purposes? By:

- Blessing His children - **Psalm 35 v 27.**

- Showing His provision & care - **Matthew 6 v 31-34.**

- (When we realise God is our source, we are released from bondage to secular wage earning only if God calls us!)

- Uniting believers to care for each other - **2 Corinthians 8 v 13-15.**

- Teaching generosity - **Luke 6 v 38.**

Quote: *"There are 3 kinds of givers: the flint, the sponge and the honeycomb. To get anything out of the flint, you must hammer it: to get anything out of the sponge you must squeeze it: but the honeycomb just overflows with its sweetness! Some people are as hard as flint: others, like sponge, yield to pressure: while others give without being asked!"*

Appendix

(These notes consist of the transcripts of a tape recording made by the Senior Minister, Pastor David Carr in 1998)

We are looking into a study on giving, tithing and money.

It's good for us to understand the Word of God and to know what the Scripture says with regards to this subject. It is funny that being British we have a different culture and often it relegates the subject to the seclusion of the private place. Like sex and politics, anger and embarrassment often result when we talk about money in public.

British people don't talk about money, yet the Bible deals with the whole perspective of finance, time, lifestyle in relationship to giving. You see giving is not just money. Giving is the whole being, it is a whole creation, and it is what we are.

All aspects of life are involved in giving, it's a heart problem not a money problem that brings resentment to the propagation of it's teaching. People get upset when they hear us talking about money and it is nothing to do with money, it is the heart.

John Wesley the great Methodist Preacher said this about money. Make all you can, save all you can, give all you can. Yet the Bible is full of warnings which many people who don't believe we should speak about money bring to our attention. It is right that we should bring it to attention; the Bible does give us warnings to mankind to keep him from being ensnared in the consequences of the worship of mammon. The word mammon means wealth and riches. Jesus says no man can serve two masters, you can't serve God and mammon. So the Word of God declares here, the whole concept of finance and money, which is another aspect of giving, can be a god in itself.

So there is God and there is mammon and you can't serve both. That does not mean that riches or wealth is sinful. It means that if you serve, submit or are besotted with it you have transferred your affections from the Lord to foreign gods. So it doesn't mean that it is sinful. But it does mean that if you worship it you have transferred your love for God to a foreign god.

That can be said of work. That can be said of leisure, marriage. The Bible would not forbid you to do these activities; on the contrary He commands us and commends that these things be done for the glory of the Lord. Imagine if Jesus said; because you might get divorced no one will marry. What would happen if God turned around and said some of you may become a workaholic, nobody will work. In fact God says that man will work by the sweat of his brow. God turned round and said that it was not good for man to be alone, so even though we can abuse anything in God, we mustn't then because we know someone who has abused it, put it as an exclusion and say, I know someone who only wants money, money, money out of God.

I know someone who only wants sex, sex, sex, well we haven't banned sex or the world would have died out years ago. We have to get this into proportion to what God is saying. So God does give us warning about money, because all money is, it's a symbol of what our heart can achieve.

A man is given a million pounds; you see his heart by the way he spends it. It is a visible evidence of the heart. God does speak about wealth, gifts and talent. These are the gifts God has given to men. Why does God give the ability to prosper? Why does God give us an ability to give? Well, it is the nature of God. But the reason we give is for the following:

To show our gratitude to Him.

How can we express our gratitude to God? There are a number of ways. The Bible says we praise, we worship, we give a clap offering. By saying that, the whole essence is, we give, we give, we give.

To give means to bestow on somebody. So the first reason that we bring our money and our tithes, our talents and we bring them to God is to show our gratitude to Him because God has given us all things. The Bible says, in the beginning was God. In the beginning was not man, it was God. God created the heavens and the earth. Without Him, nothing that was made was made. God made a beautiful garden and He put man in it.

He said, there you are man, you can have all this. The whole concept of why a man gives to God is because it is a symbol of everything that God is to Him that he repays. You see, you do a job, how does the boss show his reward to you - he gives.

Second reason that we give to God is **to worship Him.**

I have just mentioned we bring a sacrifice of praise into the House of God. Every time you come into the House of the Lord and you stand up and give a clap offering, you stand up and praise His Name. So when we bring our finances to God, we worship Him and we will see this further along.

Another reason we give is **to meet the need of others.**

The whole concept of the Bible is to give to meet the needs others.

We give to maintain the work of the ministry.

Now the reason why there is so much giving going on is because that is God's nature and we were made like God. So the more we are prepared to give in time, talent, money, praise, work, & worship denotes one of two things: either we are a driven person that we feel we must, or we are a led person because we wish.

God doesn't give because He must. God gives because He desires. Nobody made God lay His life down for us. Jesus said as He was considering the cross, Lord if there is another way out of this, do it, but not My will but Your will be done. So Jesus had an option: He could have pulled out, but Jesus had a whole desire to give; to whom? Give to Father, give to man. He was giving to Father reconciliation of a man that had sinned, and He was giving to man salvation from a God that had been sinned against. You see the whole concept of God is giving. Lets look at some of the things He gave, because it lies beyond money. **Deuteronomy 9:11** says this. God gave the 10 commandments to Moses. And why did He give them. He didn't sell them, they weren't going cheap. He gave them. Why? To condemn men - No! So that people would turn to Him and be saved.

You see men didn't know how far away from God they were until God gave the 10 commandments. Men actually said to God, why don't You tell us how good we are? When God gave Moses the 10 commandments and as soon as they heard them, the men absolutely felt wretched, because there is no way we have kept any of these. God said, I didn't give them to you to condemn you but to show you how far away from Me that you are, now come back and I will give you forgiveness. Haven't we got a good God?

In **Joshua 17:4** we read that He gave the children of Israel an inheritance amongst their fathers and brothers. Wow! Here is God who is above the universe coming to the Jews and telling them what He is going to do. I am giving you an inheritance, I am going to give you a stability, I am going to give you a lifestyle, I am going to give you a destiny, right here in the land and I'm not going to do it to split the family, I'm going to do it to make the family. So amongst your brothers and your fathers, I am going to make you secure.

God brings security into the family. He is a giver of unity. Is that good? Yes it is!

Joshua 21:43. The Lord gave Israel all the land He had promised them. Not only did He give them an inheritance; He gave them their own land. They couldn't take it, it didn't belong to them, it belonged to God. You see why would God bother to give things to man? In **verse 44**, it says **and the Lord gave them rest.** You know nobody can give you rest, only God.

In **Ruth 4:13** we see that God gave her conception. Do you know the amount of people today who can't conceive? But even those women who can conceive, it is God who gave you that ability. What a God!

1 Kings 4:29 And God gave Solomon wisdom and exceeding great understanding and largeness of heart. You see we have a concept of being British, that somehow God loves small things. That is why I preached at an Anglo Catholic Conference and when sharing that one of the priests said, In our Anglo Catholic Churches, the first thing you spot is Mary with the baby and Jesus on the cross. It was very brave of him to say, you imagine you have come from outside -you don't ask a baby for anything, you give to a baby. You don't ask a man suffering on a cross for anything because he is already suffering. What we have said to our people is, Jesus is a baby and He is suffering so don't trouble Him. We should be portraying the risen ascended Christ.

You see God gave us the baby, but men were compelled to give to the baby. We worship a God who grew bigger than a baby, a God who went to the cross, yes! He went to the grave, yes! And He was resurrected and now He sits on the right hand of God because He has ascended. That's the God that we worship.

You see He gave Solomon wisdom and exceeding great wisdom and a largeness of heart. Why would God give him minimal understanding and a small heart? Because he was British! Thank God he wasn't! And we have to get out of this attitude that God doesn't want anything big to happen to us. Solomon had such understanding that we read the Book of Proverbs, of which he wrote 3000! And 1,005 songs, that is a man who has been given a lot.

What about **Job 42:10 and the Lord restored Job's losses when he prayed for his friends.** Indeed the Lord gave Job twice as much as he had before. Now the Lord blessed the latter days of Job more than his beginning and now here's a key verse which you may not have heard or seen, and the Lord restored Job's losses when he prayed for his friends. Now he didn't pray for his friends so he could have his resources increased, you see some people say to me, well I think it's wrong teaching if you pray for your friends you'll be rich. I want to say to you folks if you pray for your friends it doesn't mean you will be rich. You see, if you do something for God to get something from God your motive is wrong. You can't use formulae to touch God. What God did, He saw this man's motives in the midst of all his disaster and in the midst of all his pain, this is what He said, **Job 42:10 and the Lord restored Job's losses when he**

prayed for his friends. God saw that this man's heart was a giving heart. You could understand Job sitting there saying, give me, give me, give me, I need, I want, I must have, but here we see Job saying, God, bless my friends and God said I can trust a man like that with a big heart. I can trust a man like that with mighty wisdom. I can trust a man like that with great wealth. Now you can confess every prayer you know, you can confess every promise given and you may never get wealth because you do not get wealth by following a formula, but by knowing the heart of God. He knows some of you He cannot trust with wealth. But He will prosper you in your heart.

To believe that everybody is entitled to great financial wealth is untrue or Paul wouldn't have said I have learnt to be content with little or with much. Some of you, if suddenly God prospered you, you would leave the faith. Somebody leaves you £300,000, you leave the faith; but notice the people God prospers financially are the people whom money doesn't touch. Speaking to a man today who has got a lot of money and he said he came to a conclusion not long ago that if God told him to leave all his big cars and his house and walk out with his wife with him with their suitcases, they'd prayed for a week and came to the conclusion that if God wanted them to leave it all behind and walk out with a suitcase, they said we'd rather walk out with a suitcase with Jesus than stay in our wealth without Him. That's prosperity. When a man does not own the house and the cars and they don't own him, but God owns them all, that's prosperity.

Psalm 24:4, He asked life from you and you gave it to him, you gave him length of days forever and forever. His glory is great in your salvation. It said, he asked life from you and God you didn't just meet what he wanted, You gave him everlasting days. Isn't God a prosperous God? Isn't God full of giving?

You see you can't stop God giving when He is on a roll. Dare I say such a thing? When God's on a roll, He's a good God. He doesn't sit there, miserly saying, I don't know if I can afford to do that this week. I told some of you that were here on Tuesday that we needed £11,000. £11,000 to meet the legal requirements of our Family Centre, I said that on Sunday morning. On Tuesday morning £20,000 came in as a cheque which means now we can put the carpet down, it's all being ordered and it's all systems go to finish it now for all the family and the youth. Yet what would you say if I told you that even before I asked that cheque was in somebody's pocket on Sunday morning in this Church, but didn't know where to give it until I declared it. Before you ask, said the Lord, it was there. Now, what a generous God. They could have made it for £11,000, but it was pressed down, shaken together and running over. Isn't God good? If God had given us £11,000 we would have rejoiced because that would have then taken away the burden of having to have all the extra fire things in, but no, He gave us another £9,000 so we could finish if off and buy all the carpets.

What a good God! If you were here and not just watching on television, you would see at this point how the people have fallen off their seats and onto the floor, they are clapping and gone so hysterical that I have had to just slow them down and we've dulled it on the sound so you can hear my voice. If you believe that, I'm lying. But, they are all excited aren't you everybody here? Yes. That's wonderful.

Now what does **John 3:16** say? **For God so loved the world,** what a God, He loves the whole world. Some of us struggle to love the person next to us. Turn round if you are here and say, I'm trying. Say that to the person next to you, and if you are at home watching this, turn round and look at the dog and say, I'm trying. **God so loved the world that He gave His only begotten Son that whosoever believes in Him should not perish but have everlasting life.** Now the word give means this, it means to bestow a gift, so God gives a gift of eternal live and we give Him a gift back of all He's given us. It means to grant a request, it means to give to one who's asking. It means to give over without any strings attached, it means to reach out to extend, so that we don't keep within our limits. It means to present it, to give over to one's love. It means it's not done through demand, but through love. It means to entrust, it means to commit, to give what is due, or obligatory. To give to someone to whom it already belongs and it already belongs to God.

So the whole nature of God is giving. Seedtime and harvest. Plant and reap. Increase, it's the law of God's nature. Now it's surprises me how many people struggle with things like finance and wealth. You know it's not sinful to plant apples. Have you ever heard someone say, I feel terrible about this, I've planted an apple tree and I just have great embarrassment, I'm going to feel very uncomfortable if it's full of apples. You say, that's stupid. When a farmer sows wheat he turns round and said to his wife, I'm going to be very embarrassed by the summer if all my field is bulging with wheat. I just feel so terrible about it I won't have the nerve to go and reap it. What about the vine? Well, with a bit of luck love we will not have any grapes this year, as I would feel embarrassed if we made a profit on the wine. No.

The natural man works hard, he plants, he keeps to everything he should do and he expects it to grow. It is not sinful to plant money; it is not sinful to plant a gift or a talent. You plant your music talent to God; if you don't expect it to grow, why did you plant it? You are an encourager and a steward. If you don't expect blessing to come out of your job, why are you doing it?

You are a mother; your husband planted a seed in you. You didn't expect it to grow; no you just expected to be permanently pregnant. But when it comes to money and of course us being British, we say well, we shouldn't really be talking about this you know. It is interesting isn't it, Jesus speaking in a parable said in **Matthew 25:15**, He gave to one man 5 talents, another 2, another 1, each according to his own ability; so according to this again, we can't make a formula out of giving. You see I have heard preachers say, if everyone stands today on my word that I am preaching and you do this everyone of you. No folks, according to Jesus, He gave unto them according to their ability to invest and their ability to control. Not everyone listening to me on the tape or sitting in this church listening to this seminar have the same abilities, but God loves us. But everyone God expects an increase. 5, 2 and 1 each according to his own ability.

Now a talent, a silver talent weighed about 100 lbs - 45 kilos. A golden talent weighed about 200 lbs. No mean stuff, it wasn't just pick up a coin. God gave to him the 500, massive amount; He said go and invest. Now if Jesus didn't believe in finance, didn't believe in giving, why would He keep giving Biblical illustrations which would bring us into sin? What did Jesus say to the man who doubled 5 who came back and said, Master, I knew you had given me this and I have been a good servant, here's 10. He said, Well done, listen to this, He said, **Well done, good and faithful servant, enter thou into the joy of the Lord.** Came to the one, who he gave 2, look he said I have got 4, He said, **Well done, good and faithful servant.** Now He didn't differentiate because he hadn't made so much, he hadn't got so much.

Let's imagine we have a worship choir here and your voice is good enough to be in it. That might be a 2 talent. You sing for God and you sing with everything you have got. Yet suppose out of that choir, you have a brilliant solo voice and you have the gifting to sing above those others. He will still say, **Well done thou good and faithful servant.** Even though you have a 5-talent ministry and the choir have 2-talent ministry, you might feel you have only a 1-talent ministry. What did he say, I don't believe in all this teaching, so I buried it in the ground and I just knew very well that, that is not exactly what you meant you are not that type of guy. You are the type of guy, that if I prosper, you are going to judge me. Jesus said, I really am, because you don't understand Me at all. He said, you sinful man. He took that which he had and gave it to the man who had 2. That would have been fairer because he knew that the man who had got 5 had made it into 10 would not be distracted by the extra one. He called him faithful, he called him servant. 2 Corinthians 9:6 says this, remember this, **whoever sows sparingly will also reap sparingly.**

Whoever sows generously, will reap generously. Each man should give what he has decided in his heart to give not reluctantly, or under compulsion for God loves a cheerful giver. You shouldn't give just because the preacher works you up, you should never give and I have been in meetings, I think we all have, where we feel sinful if we didn't. The Bible says a man must determine in his heart whatever he is doing, be it finance, be it talent, that he gives according to what is in his heart and we will see in a moment that He does give us guidelines.

This is Paul saying, remember whoever sows sparingly will reap sparingly, whoever sows generously will reap generously. For God loves a man that does it willingly, who wants to bless God. This service that you do, it goes on to say, not only supplying the needs of Gods people, in **verses 7 -12**, it is also overflowing in many expressions of thanks to God. So God says by somebody meeting the need and the by the way we have had another £330 in which has gone towards £20,330. The £330 was just as valuable, Amen. That is going to buy something we couldn't have bought without it.

And that cost the person just as much, who gave that. But it says when you gave that money on Sunday to meet that need, you were not only giving to supply that need, but in doing it you, you were giving it as an expression of thanks to God. You were saying, God you have so blessed me, I can bless others. Thank you Jesus for giving me this opportunity. Isn't that good!

So what about tithing, people ask me - that's Old Testament stuff, we shouldn't be doing that in the New Covenant. New Testament doesn't talk about tithing. Doesn't it?

Genesis 14: Abraham gave a tithe to the king, a 10th of the spoil. God gave him a great victory. Tithing started 400 years before the Mosaic Law, Abraham gave and the other leaders gave.

What does Jesus say about tithing? **Luke 11:42 But woe to you Pharisees.** Jesus says, you are big on tithing, but you have no heart in you towards justice and love. Jesus didn't say, but folks you don't need to tithe anymore, rather He said - you should put that right and give that as well as your tithe. Jesus said you should do both. Tithing is not the be all and end all of your life. Hope, love, justice, mercy, you see if you tithe and you don't have these things, you are truly legalistic. Because you are doing it to get something from God or that you are frightened of God. What Jesus is saying, is that I am not against tithing, but I want my people to tithe who are people of justice, mercy, faith, love and compassion because out of their heart comes the heart of God. So you could come here and say, oh bless God I am good Christian, I tithe, I give my 10% very week. God says if that's why you are giving it, I am not impressed. He says, give thanks with a grateful heart. When our heart is clean, then our giving is clean.

Malachi 3:10 - bring the whole tithe into the storehouse. What does that mean? It means you shouldn't give your tithe to all visiting preachers that turn up on your doorstep. There is a problem with churches often, visiting preachers come and they say, now take my leaflet and give to the ministry. Your tithe should come into your storehouse. We give gifts to these people. We do not give our tithes. Your tithe goes into the storehouse. The tithe pays the wage of the priest. You can't do that if the man doesn't belong to you and he is 2,000 miles away in Bongo, Bongo land. That is why we have a fund for people in need in our church and we give gifts out to people. The storehouse is whatever church we belong to. If we can't trust them with our tithe, then we shouldn't be there. **Bring the whole tithe into the storehouse, that there may be food in My house. Test Me in this says the Lord God Almighty and see if I will not flood open the flood gates of heaven and pour out so much blessing that you will not have room enough for it.**

Do you realise; God is saying here, **test Me!** Yet the same Scripture informs us what happens if we don't do that. He says, **will a man rob God.** Yes, He said - but you say in what way have we robbed you? In tithes and offerings. You see there is a difference between the two. You are cursed with a curse for you have robbed me, even this whole nation. Bring all the tithes into the storehouse. Now by curse, you say how can God curse me? This word curse does not mean a demonic force comes upon you, it means that if you are not putting God first, your life will be devalued and you will be living at a lower level of existence and you will not be reaching your destiny. That's a curse. **Proverbs 3:9 Honour the Lord with your wealth, with the first fruits of all your crops.** We don't give to get, that's greed; we give to bless, that's righteousness. If we have the mind of Christ and the nature of God, if we are made in His likeness, we will give with a thankful heart and it will become part of our worshipful lifestyle.

You see, we are just taking on the nature of God. According to the Scriptures, a tithe is a basic 10% of a man's income. However, if we read the Scriptures, it often says 10% of his profit. An offering is to supply a need of the ministry; a gift is a blessing for a particular project or person. There is a difference. What does God say about wealth?

Deuteronomy 8:18 Remember the Lord your God for it is He who gives you the ability to produce wealth. If wealth was not of God He wouldn't give you the ability to do it. Everything that God gives you the ability to do, you can come into bondage to, if you take God out of it. Go back to what we said, He gives you the ability to get married and you can make a god out of your marriage and not end up at the feast. He can give you the ability to own land, and spend time on it or give you the ability to earn money to buy a caravan and spend every weekend there. Does that mean caravans are sinful, that they are demonic? Does it mean if you go and sit in a caravan you are going to die? Rubbish! Everything you do you have the ability to abuse. **Deuteronomy 16:17** says, each of you must bring a gift in proportion to the way the Lord your God has blessed you.

You can't all bring the same. In the Old Testament sacrifices some bought goats and sheep and some bought doves and those who couldn't afford it joined in together and had a dove between them. God is not a God who demands you do a certain thing. He said a woman who brought her mite gave more than a man who had thousands and put hundreds in the offering. God does not count the amount at the end, He counts the heart and the head. So you see, if somebody gave that cheque for £20,000 we rejoice but out of that £330 if a young person put £3.00 in, I say, thank you Jesus. Now some could have put in that £330, they could have given their whole week's allowance. I've got news for you, even though whoever gave £20,000 will be blessed but if it's in a lesser proportion to the person who gave £30 guess who in the day of reckoning is going to be the greater blessed? **2 Corinthians 8:3** says, **for I testify that they gave as much as they were able and even beyond their ability.** Paul said in **1 Corinthians 16:2**, on **the first day of every week** which is Sunday, **each one of you should set aside a sum of money in keeping with his income.**

You see sometimes God does tell us on occasions to step beyond the boundaries. He does tell us to do that. If He does it always works. Sometimes we say, I am going to make a faith statement, but if you are going to make the faith statement don't make it, do it. You don't have to stand and declare, I'm going to do this because folks if you do it He said, don't let your left hand know what your right hand is doing. You don't have to make that statement.

I remember, I'll be careful what I say but the Church had being going for many years and somebody came and I wasn't too much up with various teachings then and they said, God told them to sell their house, give the money away because God was going to buy them one opposite twice as big so they could use it for the Lord's work and I hadn't got the spiritual authority I've got now and I thought I'm not even in this league. They stood on the Word and they say, I've heard the Word and I just didn't know what to say and I said, well you've got faith that I'm not living in. Well, that's what God has told me I'm standing on the Word and they sold their house and gave all their money away. They waited to buy the house opposite that God had promised through 3 Scriptures they were going to have and they stood on the Word and what happened? The house was sold to somebody else, they were left homeless, the Church accused us of seeing them homeless. Everybody has to put money in to buy them food. We had to rent a house and put the man on full time staff because he would have gone bankrupt. We have just got to watch that that Scripture is very good. **Each one must give a gift in proportion to the way the Lord God has blessed you** but then on rare occasions it's said here that you should set aside some and it said that they gave even more than what was normal.

You've just got to watch folks. I was with a young minister once and he said to me, I've just gone out as a faith statement and bought a very expensive new BMW. I don't have the money yet but it's a faith statement. I thought that is a presumption statement. Did God tell him to go and buy that BMW or was he doing it just to stretch his faith? No, but is it wrong to have a BMW? No. Is it wrong to drive a Rolls Royce as a Christian? No.

I hear some people say, I don't think Christians should drive Rolls Royces and that man gives virtually more away to the Kingdom of God, why shouldn't he? Nowhere in the Bible does it say you can't.

There was a very rich man, he used to build Churches and he wasn't even a Christian and he prayed because he was trying to find the philosophy of God and wanted to find God, he wasn't doing it to get to God, he just said, this is right, I should be doing it and Jesus said, this is what God said to Him, it's come up to me in heaven, I've seen your giving and heard your prayers and I like you, but before you become a Christian sell your Rolls Royce. I have no problem with Christians driving Rolls Royces as long as that is not what their aim in life is. You don't have to ride a bicycle to be holy.

You see the heart, the heart control of treasure. Our treasure holds our heart. Jesus said in **Matthew 6:21, where your treasure is there your heart will also be.**

People say to me, Pastor David I don't come to Church much because I am so busy. I say, that's good I just know where your treasure is. Well, you know I'd like to tithe but I've got everything else going on at the moment and you know I've just joined a Sports Club and I've just got to get fit, that's fine you don't have to tell me I just know where your treasure is. It's very simple that is, isn't it? Where your treasure is there your heart is. If your treasure is God that's where you are.

If you love God you'll be in His house worshipping, if you love God you'll be giving to Him. It's as simple as that: where your treasure is your heart is. People say, Pastor Dave I'd just to love to come on Tuesday's now but I'm just so busy. I was saying to somebody only not long ago, if I had your diary for a week and you had mine I reckon we would know. Let's have it for a month and I look through all your entries and you look through mine and I wonder if we could tell each other where our treasure was. It's a thought isn't? I wonder if it would say how much we talk to God in a day, how much time He talks to us? How much we give to God in time, talent and money and how much He gives to us. At the end of the week I wonder if by looking at it we would see if the Bridge Club or the brass band held our treasure? Interesting. Amen. Are you still with me? Good.

Deuteronomy 26:17 said this, an end of tithing. At the end of a tithing there was a period of a tithe and an increase of a 3rd year and they called them together and He said, look at the end of the 3rd year we want a special tithe. He said, they'll bring in the tithe within the gate. They feed the Levite; they had no inheritance like the other tribe. The Levites were the priests, they didn't have any other income and God said, you will tithe to support the men. Beside the 10th of the land they had 48 cities with the surrounding grounds. They had the best of the land. They also gave them to strangers, fatherless and widows that were within their gate. He said that if persons are within your gate you have a responsibility to bless them. Isn't that good? Isn't it wonderful when we can bless people? I was at a conference speaking only 2 weeks ago and I was talking about the servant heart, the servant spirit, and as I was saying this an alcoholic who had only been saved 2 years, brought a battered old car with him to the conference. They were in a tent, lovely wife and 2 kids, and all their clothes and everything were in the back of this battered old car and suddenly the car burst into flames and they had to pull him back from going into it. He lost the lot. The guy had hardly two halfpennies to rub together. One of the pastors said to me, Dave, he said, you know what you are preaching, he said, now is the time to share it with the people. I said, hey folks I've just been preaching about the servant heart. There is a couple out there on the hill that have lost everything, so what we want is an offering, we want clothes, we want cooking utensils. That's what we want folks, it's as simple as that. We never said, let's take the plate round, we said you can leave it at the door. We will tell you the sizes of the kid's clothes. You know at the end of that day just from that standing start and it was only from that meeting I was taking, that seminar of 200 people, they had £960 given them in cash, they had all the clothes they needed and they had all the utensils and that man went out and blessed the Lord. He went out and bought a D registered Montego estate car and you would have thought it was a brand new Rolls Royce. He stood up, we didn't know anything about his testimony. He stood up and gave his testimony and said, I was an alcoholic until 2 years ago and he couldn't cope with what the people had done. You know everybody felt good not because, aren't we good but they said, yes, we have blessed those in our gate. What a privilege it is to help people? Isn't it great?

There are people in the seminar today who are given to hospitality and by golly they bless the people, but they don't half get a blessing back. They don't do it to get blessed, they do it to bless. I am taking longer on this seminar, we normally only do 40 minutes but I believe that in many ways the Church sometimes unwittingly doesn't teach on this doctrine and I think we need to redress the balance and take a bit longer to do this, so if this tape is longer than the others so be it. **2 Chronicles 31:5** said they were called to bring a tithe, they responded immediately it said and generously with the first of their crops and grain, new wine, olive oil, money, everything else and piled them up in great heaps. Oh, how wonderful. The Living Bible said the first of these tithes arrived in June and continued till October. You see a tithe may not just be your money, it could be your food, it could be these things. You see, we turn round and say, come on folks we want to feed some poor people and you look and you say I haven't got any money, Pastor Dave but I've got a chicken out the freezer. In Africa, they can't tithe money, they haven't got it, they tithe chickens, mealy, eggs. That's great, they come to God and they give that. That's cost them more than money. They don't have money in some countries. You know, isn't great you say, God, I just can't give anything to that. Give a chicken, give a cake.

Brilliant! Isn't that wonderful. You know I've seen some people in this Church before now walking round in clothes, lovely clothes that I've seen on other people and I've had to learn never to say, hasn't Mary got a dress like that? because I have to think, it could be Mary's. They didn't have any money to give but they gave one of their best dresses away to somebody, they gave a suit. That's tithing, that's giving. I can't give £30 to that man, but I've got a suit he can have. Who knows what he'd rather have?

If he's an alcoholic he wants the booze, but if he's in need he'll have the suit. Offerings, not just tithing, but offerings. **Exodus 35:49** said this is the thing which the Lord commanded saying take from amongst you an offering to the Lord whoever is of a willing heart let him bring it in an offering to the Lord, gold, silver, bronze, a willing heart. You don't generate a wind-up. People say to me sometimes, Pastor Dave you don't put too much emphasis on giving and money and I say, no perhaps we don't and perhaps we should make it a bit higher but we did enough emphasis to get the £20,330 in, we did enough emphasis to get £10,00 in the beginning of the project and we always got the project every time we come to the people, they've risen to it and they have all done it willingly.

We've never made them feel so guilt ridden that they had to do it and they have left the Church because they couldn't afford to come again. I'd rather that happen folks than people go out guilt ridden and give because the preacher has demanded he'll be dead or paralysed next week if you don't give it. No way folks. You don't give to make me happy, you give to be obedient to God. You don't give so that David will smile next week, it's that God is worth it. Amen. We give God the first fruits.

Time doesn't permit, **Exodus 23,** we give to the poor, **Proverbs 19,** and we give to the work of God, **Exodus 35. Deuteronomy 28 said this, now it shall come to pass if you diligently obey the voice of the Lord your God to observe carefully all His commandments which I command you to today that the Lord your God will set you high above all the nations of the earth and all these blessings shall come upon you and overtake you because you obey the voice of the Lord your God.**

Isn't it great when blessings overtake you? You are not just waiting for them to get you, you are having to keep up with them. **Blessed shall you be in the city and blessed shall you be in the country,** it doesn't matter if you are a city or a country dweller. **Blessed shall be the fruit of your body, the produce of your ground, the increase of your herds, the increase of your cattle and the offspring of your flocks. Blessed shall be your baskets and your kneeling bowl, blessed shall be you when you come in and blessed shall you be when you go out.**

The Lord will cause your enemies who rise against you to be defeated before your face. They shall come out against you one way and they will flee before you seven ways. The Lord will command a blessing on you in your store houses and in all to which you set your hand and He will bless you in the land which the Lord your God is giving you. Isn't God good? It goes on to say, that **the Lord will grant you plenty of goods in the fruit of your body, in the increase of your livestock, in the produce of the ground, in the land which the Lord swore to your fathers to give you the Lord will open to you the good treasure in the heavens to give the rain to your land in its season and to bless you, your work of your hand. You shall lend to many nations but you shall not borrow.** Yes, isn't God good? As yet the world haven't give us a penny for this Church. He'll make you the head, it said not the tail. You should only be above and not beneath. **You shall not turn aside from My Words which I command you this day.** We could go on an on and we do realise that we could make a God of anything, **Ecclesiastes 5:10** said, **he who loves silver will not be satisfied with silver or he who loves abundance with increase, this is also vanity.**

You see if you worship abundance you will never be satisfied. R. T. Kendal said, we who are congenitally allergic, we English are congenitally allergic to tithing. There is something within us that tells us no, that we don't want to give. Christian giving is not a matter of finance, it's a matter of faith. Now the Church treasurer counts what we give, God counts what we keep. The Church treasurer counts what we give every

Sunday, God counts what we keep. He counts what we give, God counts what we keep. Ian Barclay the writer said this, nearly half the parables Jesus told had the use of money as their main subject.

It is sometimes said that we should give until it's hurts, but Jesus teaches that it should hurt when we cease to give. **Luke 6:38** said, **give and it shall be given unto you. Mathew 19:29, leaving all for His sake shall receive a 100 times as much now and in eternal life.**

We could say more but I think you've got the message that God is the God of giving. God is the God of abundance, God is the God of wealth and the whole essence of what I've tried to do tonight is not what are we going to get out of this? I could have given you stories of my own life how God has multiplied things. I could have given you stories of how God has really kept me and supplied every one of my needs. I could keep you till many hours in the morning telling you how after I sought first the Kingdom of God and His righteousness everything else was added unto me. I felt that by doing this, this time God was leading me today when I did this study that I was feeling God was saying to me, son keep your mind off what I do for you. I could give you testimonies that you would say, yes Oh, God, I want some of that. Instead, Jesus said, I want you to talk about giving and tithing and I want you to talk about Me. Now I know that we have touched the Scriptures that said, **will God not open up the heavens for you,** yes He will. I will tell you about when I'd got no carpet, I'd got no food on the table. I could tell you how God did it. I could tell you how I bought my house and I couldn't even afford it. God told me to buy this house when we started the Church and I got 25 years of a mortgage and 24 years 11 months to go, I couldn't afford the first payment. I faltered the first payment, I had to pay it by the Friday and on the Thursday I couldn't afford my first payment, but I was obedient to God and the next morning I opened up a letter and my solicitor - not knowing anything - had refunded me my first payment for my mortgage and by God's grace I've paid every payment ever since.

I could tell you all those stories but the emphasis then is, so you mean if I give to God I get all that? I felt that God was saying, son they don't need to know what I'll do they should trust Me for that. I want them to know that I am a giving God. I want them to know that as they become more like Me they won't have to ask, they'll give because it's My nature. And as we become more like God we can't help but give and encourage people. We give encouragement. We give help, we give service.

We have people turn round and say, you should be grateful I am doing this for you in the Church. Really? I thought you were doing it for Jesus. Well, yes I am but. No, no folks we do it for Jesus. It shall be given back to us pressed down, shaken down and running over. We give, we give. When people say to me, Dave I'm still not sure tithing is for the New Covenant. I reply, that's fine then, so can I expect far more than 10% off you now then? If you don't believe in tithing any more that means you are going to give it all because under the New Covenant if Jesus gave all for us and didn't give 10% then we are now talking about 100%. A good way of actually thinking of giving is actually repaying all our life to Him and say, Oh God, how much did you want me to have back?

I'll finish with this. A businessman was doing his business for God and God prospered him so he gave 10% to the Lord and he prospered him and so he gave 20% to the Lord and God prospered him and he gave 30% to Lord and God prospered him and he gave 40% to the Lord and God prospered him and he gave 50%, and he gave 60% and he then he gave 70% and then he gave 80% and then 90% and so he got to the point where 90% of all his substance went to God and that 10% he earned more than anybody else in that city. He actually reversed it and he kept the tithe and gave the rest to God. You say, now if I do that, no, no, you see you've missed it.

God gave him 5 talents but he called the one with the 1 a wretched man because he buried it. God would have given him an increase, He would have doubled that to 2 and He would have said exactly the same to him on the day of judgement, **well done thou good and faithful servant, enter thou into the joy of the Lord.** So what has God given you? Gifting, time, talent? People say to me, Pastor Dave how can you give time? I often say to them, I used to lecture on this. I used to say to them, hey there are very few things that every body watching this video and in this room have got in common. We are different shapes and sizes, different ages, different intellect. You know there are a number of things that really unify us in this room. One is that we are all going to die, but that is futuristic I hope. The second is everyone of us if we wake up tomorrow morning have got 24 hours. No body has got more or less unless you die. If you die and you are a Christian you've got more than 24 hours because you've got eternal life, but we all start tomorrow with 24 hours. The slate is clean, we go to bed, if we went to bed at 12 o'clock tonight and we all snuggled down in our sheets, put our heads on our pillows and went to bed. Every one of us would have the same hours tomorrow. How can you tithe that Pastor Dave they say? I can understand if you tithe money and God makes you better in something and God really blesses you, but how about hours? You just work out things that you must do, you have to go to work or school, so you say how many hours is that? Eight, so you put that down so that leaves you with eight hours to sleep. You see there is 3 periods of 8 making 24, that is why when Mars bar became a great name, the marketing man said "A Mars a day helps you work, rest and play". Eight, eight and eight. In an ideal world you work for 8, sleep for 8 and play for 8. So you then have to decide to tithe to God. If you've got to do 8 hours work you can't preach while you working, you are paid to work so that now only leaves you 16 hours. So in those 16 hours, 8 are for yourself and 8 are for sleep. So if you need to tithe to God you decide then what you are going to give Him. So say you've got 16 hours a day, you would give 1.6 hours of day to God.

I am sure most of us don't do that. You say, Pastor Dave I couldn't afford to do that, I can't even give Him 10 minutes - that's why you are busy doing nothing working the whole day through trying to find lots of things not to do. You know I actually started tithing time just before I started this Church and I met a man at this Anglo-Catholic Conference and he hadn't seen me for 20 years and he used to work at the company I worked at and he said, David Carr, I only became a Christian last year, I remember you. I have always wanted to ask you a question when I wasn't a Christian and I still do. How could you run a very successful business, run a Church, run a home, go on television and go round the world preaching? How could you do that when I could only do one job? I replied, quite easy, I used to tithe my time to God and found that I could do more in 3 days at work than men did in a fortnight. I used to do more business in one week than they did in a month. A boss when you are in selling, doesn't matter how many hours you do, he wants to know, can you do the business? So I was one of the few men who spoke at a major conference at the Barbican Centre and the man said at the end of my lecture when I said I don't work any weekends, work any nights, I only work Monday, Tuesday, Thursday, Friday and I was one of the top men in Britain. He stood up there and he said, and I told them why, because I tithed my time to God. I didn't give God time and live off the state. If you are really tithing it you are blessed.

WEEK 5
MINISTRY OPPORTUNITIES & SERVING

HOW TO BE USEFUL TO GOD
Identifying Your Ministry Gifts

What Are Ministry Gifts?

It becomes clear when we read the New Testament that God does not expect any believer to live in isolation. He expects us to be in fellowship with one another.

Matthew 18:19-20 *"Again, I say to you that if two of you on earth agree concerning anything that they ask, it will be done for them by My Father in heaven. For where two or three are gathered together in My name, I am there in the midst of them".*

Romans 12:4-5 *"For as we have many members in one body, but all the members do not have the same function, so we, being many, are one body in Christ, and individually members of one another".*

Hebrews 10:24-25 *"And let us consider one another in order to stir up love and good works, not forsaking the assembling of ourselves together, as is the manner of some, but exhorting one another, and so much the more as you see the Day approaching".*

1 Corinthians 12:27 *"Now you are the body of Christ, and members individually".*

We become members of Christ's body, or the Church, at the moment of our conversion - this is an automatic process. Our main purpose in the Church is to build up the body.

Ephesians 4:12 *"For the equipping of the saints for the work of ministry, for the edifying of the body of Christ".*

Ephesians 4:16   *"From whom the whole body, joined and knit together by what every joint supplies, according to the effective working by which every part does its share, causes growth of the body for the edifying of itself in love".*

Romans 14:19   *"Therefore let us pursue the things which make for peace and the things by which one may edify another".*

Jude 20   *"But you, beloved, building yourselves up on your most holy faith, praying in the Holy Spirit".*

1 Thessalonians 5:11 *"Therefore comfort each another and edify one another, just as you also are doing".*

1 Corinthians 14:16 *"Otherwise, if you bless with your spirit, how will he who occupies the place of the uninformed say 'Amen' at your giving of thanks, since he does not understand what you say?".*

The Lord places each one of us within the Church to perform a task, or tasks, which He has designed specifically for us, and for which He has equipped us, i.e. we are definitely capable of doing the task(s) He has given us. Performing that task to the best of our ability is the calling of every Christian. Please note that the Lord knows the task(s) He wants us to perform before He saves us: indeed He has been preparing us throughout our lives for these very tasks. N.B. This is not the reason He saves us! We are saved above all else because He loves us!

For the Church to function at its most effective every believer must carry out the task(s) God has given them. This is because each task requires different gifts and that is why God gives each believer a different combination of gifts - to seek the precise combination of gifts that God has given to another believer is a mistake: we do not need somebody else's combination of gifts - we need the combination which the Lord has given us.

What Are The Gifts That God Gives Us To Help Us To Carry Out Our Task(s)?

They are a combination of natural gifts (or talents) and supernatural or spiritual gifts: every believer has both natural and supernatural gifts, because every believer needs a combination of both of these in order to be able successfully to carry out their God-given task(s).

But what are supernatural or spiritual gifts, and how do they differ from natural gifts (or talents)?

A supernatural or spiritual gift can be explained in a number of ways, each of which attempts to make the definition clearer. It is

a. A God given ability designed to help us carry out our Christian service.

b. The spiritual motivation within us, which prompts us to serve God in certain ways.

c. The inner drive found only in believers, i.e. born-again Christians, which enables them to function in the Church in the way that the Lord intends.

A supernatural or spiritual gift is not the same as a natural gift or talent: everyone has natural gifts but only believers have spiritual gifts.

The Lord gives each one of us at least one spiritual gift.

Very often He takes a natural gift and increases or intensifies it so that it becomes a spiritual urge or motivation with the potential which God can use to make a significant contribution to the ministry of the Church.

So, in a nutshell, what are we saying?

The gifts of the Holy Spirit are God's power in action. They will become manifest in our lives when we find ourselves in circumstances where their working is very much needed. As God equips us by His Holy Spirit He will lift us beyond the limits of our own weaknesses, constraints or talents. We are then equipped to carry out the will of God. Without these gifts we live and function only at the level of our natural abilities, talents and strengths. With the gifts of the Holy Spirit we function at the level of God's ability, insight and potential. What a difference!

What Are My Ministry Gifts?

We shall concentrate exclusively on the list found in **Romans 12:6-8** in the belief the every believer possesses at least one of these gifts:

Romans 12:6-8 *"Having then gifts differing according to the grace that is given to us, let us use them: if prophecy, let us prophesy in proportion to our faith; or ministry, let us use it in our ministering; he who teaches, in teaching; he who exhorts, in exhortation; he who gives, with liberality; he who leads, with diligence; he who shows mercy, with cheerfulness".*

1 Corinthians 7:7 *"For I wish that all men were as I myself. But each one has his own gift from God, one in this manner and another in that".*

1 Peter 4:10   *"As each one has received a gift, minister it to one another, as good stewards of the manifold grace of God".*

How Can We Discover Which One?

There are a number of thoughts we need to consider before we can complete this task:

1. **Knowing the meaning of the gifts:** we need to study each gift in turn to ensure that we understand fully what it means; then we are more likely to recognise our own gifting.

2. **Pray:** we must seek guidance from the Lord and ask Him to help us.

3. **Be aware of your natural gifts/talents:** very often your main spiritual gift is a heightened natural gift, i.e. our natural gifts or talents are very often the natural wrapping in which a spiritual gift may be deposited. God very often places a spiritual gift on top of a natural gift and so we need to fully understand which natural gifts we possess before we can be certain to discern our spiritual gifts.

4. **Work through the list in Romans 12 one at a time:** as you work through the list slowly and prayerfully ask the Lord to witness to your heart just what gifts (or gifts) He has given you. You may need to do this more than once before you can be certain of the Lord's answer.

5. **The discernment of others:** very often other believers will see a spiritual gift in your life before you do: seek the confirmation of others, therefore, but also be willing to encourage others when you see a gift at work in their lives. It is possible for one believer to pray for, and over, another believer, so that the latter will find his/her spiritual gifting.

6. **Gifts make room for themselves:** there is no need to rush around the church building telling everyone which gift you possess! Do not begin to worry if your gift is not immediately recognised and then used in the main assembly, wait for God to create the opportunities for you to use your gift(s).

7. **Joy comes through using the gift:** the inner joy we experience when we use our spiritual gift is often the best sign that we possess that particular gift. However, the joy only comes when we use the gift!

2 Timothy 1:6   *"Therefore I remind you to stir up the gift of God which is in you through the laying on of my hands".*

1 Timothy 4:14   *"Do not neglect the gift that is in you, which was given you by prophecy with the laying on of the hands of the presbytery".*

8. **Whether or not you have a particular gift God still expects us to obey His commands:** thus all believers are commanded to give tithes, gifts and offerings, irrespective of whether or not we have the gift of "giving".

9. **Once God gives a gift He does not take it back:**

   Romans 11:29 *"For the gifts and the calling of God are irrevocable".*

10. **Never become jealous and/or envious of others gifts and/or ministries:** God has not called us to copy another person but to be like Jesus. The combination of gifts that God gives to each person is unique because we are all unique individuals. Therefore, be content with that which the Lord has given you; furthermore, look for every opportunity to encourage others in the use of their gifts.

Romans 12:6-8 *"Having then gifts differing according to the grace that is given to us, let us use them: if prophecy, let us prophesy in proportion to our faith; or ministry, let us use it in our ministering; he who teaches, in teaching; he who exhorts, in exhortation; he who gives, with liberality; he who leads, with diligence; he who shows mercy, with cheerfulness".*

There are seven gifts listed here (and two more elsewhere), namely:

1. **Prophecy:** The God-given ability to present truth. A persuasiveness and power in speech that brings to light things which were previously concealed. The ability to supernaturally convey God's message for the moment in the language of the speaker and the hearers. It is used to bring a message of edification (building up), exhortation (encouraging), or comfort to God's people at specific times. The ability to speak clearly, but also the ability to hear what God is saying with the urge to pass it on. At its best, prophecy has no connection with human thought, reasoning or intellect. It is inspired utterance not born of intellect or study.

2. **Serving or ministering:** demonstrating love by meeting practical needs so that others can be freed for service. An ability to detect the needs of another and to overlook personal comfort so that the needs of others can be met. The ability to give practical assistance. The person who has this gift will demonstrate a deep concern and desire to help another brother or sister in practical ways so that they can be more effective in their ministry. Manifesting a deep concern for the spiritual growth of others who, owing to difficult situations and circumstances, find the Christian life an uphill climb.

3. **Teaching:** clarifying the truth by expounding the meaning of Scripture by ensuring the accuracy of the context. An ability to research and unearth facts from Scripture and to compare one Scripture with another so that the truth can be presented in a proper perspective. This involves diligence, fervency in study and careful research.

The ability to communicate intelligibly with others and to impart to others a right understanding of the Bible's truths having regard to the right interpretation of words and metaphors. Put simply - people with this gift have the God-given ability to make people understand what God is saying and what His purpose is.

4. **Exhorting and encouraging:** sometimes known as stimulating the faith of others. Shown by a spiritual eagerness to encourage others in the faith, possibly through counselling. It involves an ability to come alongside a weaker Christian to help, strengthen and direct that person toward the Scriptural solution to the problems. The ability to say the right words and to minister to others in such a way that these people go forward in their Christian walk. Sharing experiences of God's goodness and the richness of His promises in Scripture. The ability to encourage others to specific action towards definite goals.

5. **Giving or sharing:** this carries the concept of a God-given ability to organise one's personal affairs so as to be able to enrich the work of God with material assets. A person with this gift will be clear thinking in relationship to the wise use and distribution of money. Demonstrating a high degree of wisdom to make quick and sound decisions about the right use of money. The inclination to share one's good things. The urge to give regularly and generously to the work of the Lord. It does not presuppose that the person with this gift is materially rich. Joyfully entrusting personal assets or possessions to others for the work of the ministry. An ability to organise personal business. An ability to invest wisely.

6. **Ruling or leading:** a God-given ability to preside over or lead others by co-ordinating their activities for the achievement of common goals. A person so gifted is able to look ahead and distinguish the major objectives before others see them, and to clarify these objectives for others. Seeing the future consequences of one's actions. The ability to lead in such a way that others follow. The ability to plan, organise and administer with wisdom, fairness and efficiency.

7. **Showing mercy:** empathising by an ability to identify with and comfort those in distress. An ability to sympathise deeply with the misfortunes of others. Mentally and emotionally relating with, and giving aid to, others. Entering into the mental and emotional needs of others and relating to them in a meaningful way. The ability of human compassion and being cheerful at the same time. As we seek God in this He will enable us to fulfil our destiny in the body of Christ. The Church will only grow in quantity and quality as each of us pull our weight and fulfil the function God has given us. Then and only then will the Church here at Renewal become the body that is truly the expression of Jesus on earth. Awesome!

These seven are generally regarded as the main spiritual gifts given by the Father, and so we shall be concentrating on them. However, there are at least two others that we shall look at briefly, namely:

8. **Celibacy: 1 Corinthians 7:7 "For I wish that all men were even as I myself. But each one has his own gift from God, one in this manner and another in that".** A God-given ability to resolve not to marry so that the individual can more fully serve the Lord.

9. **Speaking: 1 Peter 4:10-11 "As each one has received a gift, minister it to one another, as good stewards of the manifold grace of God. If anyone speaks, let him speak as the oracles of God. If anyone ministers, let him do it as with the ability which God supplies, that in all things God may be glorified through Jesus Christ, to whom belong the glory and the dominion forever and ever. Amen".** An ability to use the correct words to suit any particular circumstance so that others understand what is being said so that there is no ambiguity.

Exercise To Discover Your Ministry Gifts

1. I enjoy presenting God's truth in an inspired and enthusiastic way.

2. I am always ready to overlook my own personal comfort in order that the needs of others may be met.

3. I find great delight in explaining the truth of a Bible text (verse) within its context.

4. I am able to verbally encourage those who waver and who are spiritually troubled.

5. I am able to manage my financial affairs efficiently so that I can give generously to the Lord's work.

6. I find it easy to delegate (give to others) responsibility and organise others towards spiritual achievement.

7. I readily find myself sympathising with the misfortunes of others.

8. I am conscious of a persuasiveness of speech when encouraging people to examine their spiritual motives.

9. I have the knack of making people feel at home.

10. I delight in digging out facts concerning the Bible so that I can pass them on to others.

11. I have a deep concern to encourage people toward spiritual growth and achievement.

12. I am cheerful about giving material assets (money) so that the Lord's work can be furthered.

13. I am able effectively to supervise the activities of others.

14. I enjoy visiting those in hospital, or the "shut in's."

15. I am able to present the Word of God to a congregation of people with clarity and conviction.

16. I am happy when asked to assist others in the Lord's work, without necessarily being appointed to a leadership position.

17. I am concerned that truth should be presented in a clear fashion with proper attention to the meaning of words.

18. I am at my best when treating those who are spiritually hurt.

19. I have no problem in joyfully entrusting my assets (money) to others for the work of the ministry.

20. I am able to plan the actions of others with ease and supply them with details which will enable them to work effectively.

21. I have a great concern for those involved in trouble.

22. I find myself preaching for a response whenever I present the truths of the Word of God.

23. I delight in providing a gracious haven (comfortable home) for guests.

24. I am diligent (industrious, steady in application) in my study of the Bible and give careful attention to necessary research.

25. I am able to help those who need counselling over personal problems.

26. I am concerned over the question of financial assistance being available for all sections of the Church.

27. I am deeply sensitive to the need of a smooth running administration so that every phase of activity is carried out decently and in order.

28. I work happily with those who are ignored by the majority.

29. I find my preaching brings people to a definite point of decision.

30. I enjoy taking the load from key people so that they can put more effort into their own particular task.

31. I am able to explain well how the Bible fits together.

32. I am acutely aware of the things that hold people back in their spiritual development and long to help them overcome their problems.

33. I am careful with money and continually pray over its proper distribution in the work of the Lord.

34. I know where I am going and am able to take others with me.

35. I am able to relate to others emotionally and am quick to help when help is needed.

Read through the 35 statements above and then using the chart below score each statement in the following way: is this statement true in my spiritual life and experience?

Greatly = 3;   Some = 2;   Little = 1;   Not at all = 0.

Once you have scored all 35 statements, add together the scores in the horizontal rows: enter your score **ABOVE** the line in the box marked **TOTAL:** at the moment **PLEASE DO NOT WRITE BELOW the line in the box marked TOTAL.** After we have all finished we shall interpret the results together. Please answer as honestly as you can.

						ROW TOTAL
ROW	1	8	15	22	29	_____
ROW	2	9	16	23	30	_____
ROW	3	10	17	24	31	_____
ROW	4	11	18	25	32	_____
ROW	5	12	19	26	33	_____
ROW	6	13	20	27	34	_____
ROW	7	14	21	28	35	_____

To help us in our understanding of the type and operation of these ministry gifts, here are some Scripture references.

- **PROPHECY**

    Ezekiel *(Ezekiel 14)*

    Peter *(Acts 2 and 5)*

- **SERVING OR MINISTERING**

    Jesus *(John 13)*

    Dorcas *(Acts 9)*

    Stephen *(Acts 6)*

- **TEACHING**

    Jesus *(Matthew 5)*

    Apollos *(Acts 18)*

    Paul *(2 Timothy 1:11)*

- **EXHORTING AND ENCOURAGING**

    Paul and Barnabas *(Acts 14:21)*

- **GIVING OR SHARING**

    Church in Macedonia *(2 Corinthians 8:1)*

    Barnabas *(Acts 4:36-37)*

- **RULING OR LEADING**

    Joseph *(Acts 7:9-10)*

    Elders *(1 Timothy 5:17)*

    Deacons *(I Timothy 3:12)*

- **SHOWING MERCY**

    Samaritan *(Luke 10:34)*

    Jesus *(Matthew 8:1; John 8:8)*

    Barnabas *(Acts 9:26-27)*

Appendix

(These notes consist of the transcripts of a tape recording made by the Senior Minister, Pastor David Carr, in 1998)

'What is the Church?' Often people ask, what Church do you belong to? And where is your Church? It's interesting when you start reading the Bible and especially the Words of Jesus. Jesus only mentions the Church once of any significance. Jesus said, *I will build My Church and the gates of hell shall not prevail.*

Now the word Church is mentioned in the Letters 92 times and they actually talk not about a building, or a denomination, or a grouping, but about the people who are called out. The word is *ecclesia,* it means to be called out of. Somehow in history we have taken our eyes off that and we have transferred it to the building. We have transferred it to the denomination. So you have the Church of England, The Roman Catholic Church, the Elim Pentecostal Church, the Faith Church. The Bible tells us that John the Baptist came preaching repentance in the Kingdom of God and Jesus came preaching repentance in the Kingdom of God.

Now to preach the Church in that sense is wrong because the Church are those people who have been born into the Kingdom of God and God has brought them together to become His bride. They are a group of people that God had ordained from all colours, all nations, all denominations that will be the bride of Christ. So when Jesus said, *I will build My Church and the gates of hell shall not prevail against them* often people have missed it by a thousand miles. All through the Bible, e.g. if you look through Matthew, Jesus talks about the Kingdom of God. Notice we said He only makes one major reference to Church.

In *Matthew Chapter 13*, He said *because it has been given to you to know the mysteries of the Kingdom of heaven.* In *verse 19, when anyone hears the Word of the Kingdom. Verse 24, another parable He put forth to them saying, the Kingdom of heaven is like a man who sowed good seed in a field.* By *verse 31,* He said *the Kingdom of heaven is like a mustard seed which a man took and sowed in his field. Verse 33, another parable He spoke to them, the Kingdom of heaven is like leaven which a woman took and hid in three measures. Verse 38 He said the field is the Word, the good seed are the sons of the Kingdom. Verse 43, He said, then the righteous will shine forth as the Son in the Kingdom of their Father. Verse 44, again the Kingdom of heaven is like treasure hidden in a field. Verse 45, again the Kingdom of heaven is like a merchant seeking beautiful pearls. Verse 47, again the Kingdom of heaven is like a dragnet that was cast into the sea and gathered some of every kind. Verse 52, therefore every scribe instructing concerning the Kingdom of heaven is like a householder who brings out of his treasure things new and old.*

Even in the Lord's Prayer the Kingdom of God is mentioned twice. It said, **Thy Kingdom come, Thy will be done on earth as it is in heaven.** Then He finishes off by saying, **for Thine is the Kingdom, the power and the glory.** So the whole concept of God is that He's come to preach a Kingdom and a Kingdom is the rule of the King, pretty obvious isn't it? We are called in this country at the moment, a United Kingdom because it's based round a monarch. So on your passport it says the United Kingdom of Great Britain and Northern Ireland.

Therefore the Church comes out of the Kingdom, so you can actually come to Church and not be Church. That's why people say to me, why is the Church called the Renewal Christian Centre? If you called it Church you wouldn't have so much confusion and I think the reason why I did that was because I don't want the people to associate the building as Church, or everything's centred round the building, but Jesus taught the Church should go out to the people. **Go into all the world and preach the Gospel to every creature and lo, I am with you always.** You see, the Church comes out of that Kingdom.

Let me explain that to you. As we begin to preach the Words of Jesus, because Jesus is the King, we have found over the last few weeks on the Sundays that the numbers have been growing, growing, growing because what we are doing is proclaiming that you need to know the King and you need to allow His rule to come into your life. Jesus said, when you know Me the Kingdom of God is within you. Now, once the Kingdom of God is within us and we are part of this new life, this new nation, we become a royal priesthood, a holy nation, then God builds us into His Church. Now think about it, if God builds His Church and we are not building our Church, we don't have to then get books on Church growth. You see when we start to build our Church, it's our Church, but Jesus said, **I will build My Church and the gates of hell shall not prevail.** You might think we're playing on words, but there is a subtle difference when we start building our Church and when we start putting a big emphasis on our Church and there's nothing wrong in loving the group of people who you are with, that's fine and that's right.

What happens is then we become protective, we become obsessive, then there's this big battle going on for position and rank. So what happens is we go into the world and we preach the Kingdom of God because that's what Jesus came to do and we preached the Kingdom of God because that's what Jesus came to do and we preached the Kingdom of God because that's what John came to do and we preached the Kingdom of God because that's what Peter did on the day of Pentecost.

As soon as the Church was born in **Acts 2** the first thing they did was to preach the Kingdom of God. You see the Church is the agency whereby the Kingdom is preached and as we begin to preach the Kingdom of God, which is to restore man, to forgive man, to heal man, then God begins to build His Church. Now isn't it wonderful when we have to stop building our Church and we can let God build His own and any group of people who allow God to build His Church, then don't have to worry, even though we might have problems, even though there may be schisms come in and the Bible said, and Paul said, that we are to be like a guardian shepherd watching the wolves and making sure false prophets don't come in. Then if it's God's Church whoever lays a hand against us is fighting against God.

However, if we set out to build a Church and if we set out to grow it - you see a human man can grow a human Church; if a man's got enough ingenuity, if he's got enough charisma, he's got enough help and enough money, any man can build a Church on basic psychological theology. He can say the right things in the right way, put on the right programme for the right time and get the right people, but he can't keep them.

When we start preaching the King and we starting preaching the Kingdom of God, or as I call it the "red bits", which are the Words of Jesus, then you'll suddenly find then that rather than following a man and rather than being obsessed on a doctrine, you'll suddenly then find that you are hooked on the Words of God. Jesus Himself said, My Words when they dwell in you will bless you richly, so as we begin to become children of the Kingdom, so what happens is that God wonderfully creates His Church. Now the Church are the called out ones, the ecclesia. Jesus said, let them be in the world but not of it. He calls us out, yet the Kingdom means we go in.

This is why so often in Church everything is come in, come in, come in, when Jesus said to the Church, no come out of the world so you don't live like the world, but go and take the message of the Kingdom back into the world. You know I said at a Leader's Seminar this Monday, we were looking at the Kingdom with the Church Leaders here, we had a training night and I said it's interesting isn't it that the Church prepares the bride for Christ yet the Kingdom saves the prostitute from the gutter.

The Kingdom of God is for the prostitute. So here's Jesus turning round to the woman, the King, and He said, **give me to drink** and she said, if only you knew who you were speaking to and He said, if only you knew who you were speaking to I would give you rivers of living water. She drank and He said, where is your husband? She said, I have no husband. He said, you've said right, you've had five and the man you are living with is not your own. She repented, she found the living waters. She went back, saw the men she had slept with, brought them back, they believed because they saw the change in her life and they said, now we believe because we have seen You for ourselves.

These men had been impacted by the King and the teaching of the Kingdom of God, yet on the day of Pentecost those men were forged into the Church. I don't know if I'm making myself understood by you, so you can actually be in Church but not be in the Kingdom. You can come to Church for thirty years, you can be baptised and christened, yet not be part of the Church. You can actually come to Church and not be part of the Kingdom. That's why Jesus said, **many will come and will say, did** *we not teach in our streets, have we not prophesied in your Name, have we not cast out evil spirits and He said, I don't know you.* You can be absorbed into the Church structure but not be part of the Church, the bride of Christ.

It's interesting isn't it that the Church is getting ready to go, yet the Kingdom of God is being prepared to come. You see the Lord's Prayer said, **Thy Kingdom come on earth as it is in heaven,** but the bride, which is the Church, is waiting to go home. When the trump of the Lord shall sound the dead in Christ shall be raised into incorruption and those who remain will be changed and be taken to meet Him in the air. That's exciting! So the whole essence of being part of God's Church is that He's coming for us, a bridegroom for the bride. When He comes, we'll be without spot, which is immaturity, or wrinkle, which is old age, without spot or blemish.

So the Church is looking to go, the Kingdom is looking to come. Pray this prayer He said, **Thy Kingdom come, Thy will be done on earth as it is in heaven.** You see the Kingdom of God and the Church, one is born out of the other. The Church is born out of the Kingdom and then the Church preaches the Kingdom, but there is in that sense a distinct difference. When we come together to worship, we are the preparation of a bride, but when the Church goes out and preaches it's to the rescue of the prostitute. Do you understand the difference? So often people are preaching Church when they should be preaching Kingdom and they are not living Church when they should.

So Church are those who love God, so you see in a sense you are not joining this Church; as you watch this video you say to yourself, I think I could get along with these people, warts and all even though the Pastor has passed his sell by date, I think I could cope. You say, I would really like to belong to that Church but realise this, you are not belonging to this fabric and this building. You are not belonging to a name at the front. If you are, you must be a person who loves God, who has been born of His Spirit, a person who has stood and been baptised in water, because the Bible said and Jesus said, **repent and be converted and be baptised**. So there is an obedient act there and we must be people who have a love one for each other and in that sense you might want to join this group of people, this fellowship, this centre. Yet, only God joins you to His Church, because it's His Church. So the Church is not the Renewal Christian Centre, that may well be part of it.

Now within His Church what does He put within the ministry? Now the word ministry means to serve or to be a servant. It's so interesting, so often people say I want to go into full-time ministry, we feel if we are not fulfilled unless we are full-time. The Bible doesn't talk about full-time ministry, Paul turns round and says, if a man chooses to take a salary make sure you are not stingy. It's good to preach this. Make sure you are not stingy, he said, make sure you don't hold it back in case the man spends all the time worrying about his bills he can't preach the Word. He said, give him a double honour so that man can just spend time in the Word of God. Now, of course I used to preach this because I used to have my own business until five years ago anyway, so I used to preach this while the Church never paid me. For twenty one of the twenty six years it has been going the Church never paid me a cent, so I could preach this and now that I am full time I let somebody else preach it so it doesn't look as if I am looking for a pay rise.

So God is good but I want to say this to you, ministry is not an elevated group of men who have a special anointing. Ministry is what we are first to God. The Psalmist said, **come bless the Lord all you servants of the Lord who stand by night in the house of the Lord.** Every person who loves God has a ministry. Now you could not believe in the natural that we could bless God because a lot of our prayers are bless me, bless me, bless my kids, the dog, you know the cat, that makes three. God bless me. Help me, help me Jesus, help me.

Who has ever thought, what you give a man at Christmas who has got everything? What can you give to God who made everything? Then the Bible says, **I will bless the Lord at all times, His praise shall continually be in my mouth,** which means the Bible is either true or wrong and it's true. So we can bless God. Now what does the word bless mean? It means to evoke happiness upon. So a child that has no money, no sense and no education can be a blessing to his parents. He can really bring a blessing. How often have those of us who have children said, you know they are a really blessing that baby. They have really bought a blessing into my heart. They have really made me happy and you know the Bible said, **it's a delight to do Your will oh God,** and as we begin to do things in our life and be things to God that exalt God and not us, then God is blessed. Now I am thrilled about that. That we can actually give God something, it just blows me away. So we are all here to minister.

Now in the Old Covenant, of course, they had selected priests because everything in the Old Testament was symbolic and the priests in that day used to go and they would be a separated man and he would go on behalf of the people. There was a High Priest and he used to go through a ceremonial washing and he used to put a breast plate on and he used to have a linen gown, he used to have a method and he used to take the blood which was representing, he was a representative of Christ who would come, and he used to put the blood on his thumb and on his big toe and on the lobe of his ear. He used to have a cord round him, he used to have pomegranates and bells around the edge of his robe. He used to go inside the Holy of Holies through the curtain and he would have a rope round him. They would send him in there so that he would come and he would sprinkle the blood and he would come to the Mercy Seat and he would say, God we are all sinners, but he used to purify himself before he went in, he would wash himself and then he would go there and he would say, Father please accept the sacrifice, the shedding of the blood of the lamb. He used to take the doves, the turtle doves and he would bring these in and say, God please forgive us for we have been sinners and they would listen and if the gown wasn't moving and if this man has gone in unrighteously and hadn't cleansed himself and God had judged his unrighteousness (you can't stand before God if you are unclean) and he died, they couldn't go in to get him out because if they went in they would die. So they would pull him out by the rope. But wasn't it wonderful when Jesus Christ came and the Bible says, He is our great High Priest, He tore the veil. Remember on the Cross He said, it was rendered. It was a good word. It just ripped. Man goes like that, God goes like that. He rips it open and so God said, isn't it wonderful.

Jesus our great High Priest now, who was clean without going through the ceremony, who took His blood upon Himself, our blood upon Himself, just like the priest, went before His Father and said, Lord those that you have given Me, I've lost none save the son of perdition, Judas who killed himself, who wouldn't repent. If he had called on God he would have been received as well. Only lost one. Isn't that wonderful! Those who genuinely seek Jesus, you will not be lost. I have lost none.

Well you wouldn't expect God to lose anybody because to lose something is a defect within me. If I lose my keys it's because I am forgetful. God never ever forgets. People say, He does, He forgets our sin. No, He doesn't, He chooses to remember them no more. It takes a man's will to choose not to remember, it takes a fool to forget. God's no fool. In fact we are the fools because the Bible says, **forget not all His benefits, in all your ways acknowledge Him, He will direct your path.** God said, a man is a fool if he doesn't believe in God. **A fool said in his heart, there is no God.** God does not forget, He remembers them no more.

Just like God makes a conscious decision to love us. He makes a conscious decision to forgive us and He makes a conscious decision not to remember. What a great God we've got! I am excited about that. I'm getting so excited I could dance but for the cameras I won't. So now we see in the New Covenant that God calls us - and Luther brought this out and of course we mustn't go over the top and you can take all truth to excess and he said, on that basis we are all a royal priesthood, we are all believer priests, but if that is the case, we have a responsibility not to do our own thing.

No priest did their own thing and in the charismatic, Pentecostal, evangelical world today Churches have been decimated because people do that which seems right in their own heart. I've got a prophecy, I've got this. God said this, 'I'm a priest', I can sit at home, I don't need Church, I can read my own word. What they've done is used that belief to become rebellious to the body of Christ. Now God does say in a sense, that we can all stand boldly before Him and He says, **I wish you all prophesied** but then He gave ministry gifts which we believe in, in this Church, which is for the edifying and that word edify means to build up into maturity, of the Church.

So I was an evangelist before I became a pastor, but I based myself in a Church and become under the submission of an eldership. My personal view, and you might not necessarily agree, I don't believe in para-Church organisations. I don't believe in Church organisations that do not have a Church base. About Peter, who was the first preacher, God said, I will build My Church, Peter and your ministry, there's the gates, these are the keys to the Kingdom, not to your Church but to the Kingdom. God won't give His keys away, they are His Church don't forget. There's the keys to the Kingdom and when Peter preached and in two sermons 8,000 people got saved. Even this man who was apostolic, the only apostle to stand and preach on the day of Pentecost, he moved under the power of God, went back to elders of Jerusalem and submitted why Cornelius had been filled with the Spirit and baptised. He didn't say hey, hey I am the apostle round here man, you all submit to me, because the gifts, the ministry gifts in the Church are about servanthood, not being dictatorial. Do you understand what I am saying? They are to build the Church up, not to keep the Church down. They are there to lift up, not to put down. Yes, they have to discipline, but the Bible says, parents are supposed to discipline, but surely parents aren't then dictatorial. You know, we are getting legalistic. Why? Because Dad said, go to bed. If it's for your benefit and it's right, then you obey. No, it's not, well we like it so we obey but we disagree, we don't.

Is it Biblical? Yes, obey because Jesus said these people become a covering. See, the greatest punishment that God can give a person is to ex-communicate them from a Church. Now sometimes men do it when they shouldn't and sometimes men don't when they should. You see, why we should belong to the Church and why we should belong to a local fellowship, is because God puts protections and the Bible said that the Church is the covering and they are the first point of covering in our life. Then comes Christ who is the Head, then comes Father. Now it means that if Christ is the Head of the Church and we sin and we will not take counsel and we sin and we are removed and put outside of that Church, then we don't have the protection of God and the Devil, just like when an animal comes aside from the herd, can go straight for it and God said, I stand back hoping that by molesting you he will drive you back into repentance. That's why on the eight or nine occasions in twenty-five years I have ex-communicated people - and they have been people for gross sin who have not repented or will wish to and have taken no instruction - I have had to hand them over so the Devil will go for them to drive them back to repentance. It's a very difficult thing. So, we belong to a fellowship for mutual building in God and for discipline and for protection.

So there are various gifts in the Church and I believe even though a lot of these gifts are external, they should always be based internally. You see, there are the apostles and of course what happens with human thinking is we tend to put them in the order apostles, prophets, evangelists, teachers, pastors. God is never, gold, silver, bronze. When we think of the triune God, Father, Son and Holy Spirit, it is not Father above the Son who is then above the Holy Spirit, but it's Father, Son and Holy Spirit who are co-equal. Dare I say in such a crude example, they all won the gold. They were level pegging when they came past the post, so the three gold medals were given. It's not the pecking order of gold, silver, bronze and we tend to think, well one day if I become an apostle I've arrived. Shandar man's here. No. An apostle is no higher than a pastor. In fact in the local Church the pastor and his eldership are always the ultimate authority.

So when I go out, I don't know what I really am now, because I'm all things to all men. I go to some Churches and they say, an apostle's come. I go to others and they say, here comes a prophet. I go to others and they say, teacher, which is a great shock to me. Others say, he's an evangelist and others say oh what a pastor. When Paul says, *I am all things to all men,* that's what he meant. He didn't mean I am a compromise to the compromised, to the effeminate I am effeminate, to the drunk I'm a drunk. He said, whatever you see me to be I am. If you see an apostolic thing, because Paul went on to say, I know I am not an apostle to you all because some of you don't accept me as an apostle, but I am an apostle of Jesus Christ. So I think it's wonderful when other people know me as the Senior Pastor; it used to be because I was the leading pastor, now it's because of my age! They think, he must be senior looking at his age. Then I don't have a card with my gifting on. So I haven't got, "prophet to the nations", "apostle to the area", "evangelist to the country". It's wonderful not having to carry a title and whatever the people see me to be, so tomorrow night I'm speaking to leaders up in Darlington, up in the North and stopping overnight and doing another seminar for leaders and coming down Saturday morning and Sunday morning I come in, I'm the pastor.

I am going to Zimbabwe speaking to 1,000 pastors, I don't know what they see me, they might see me as prophetic. It matters not. Now when I go to Cape Town they see me as a father and I go there and I give them Spiritual fathership. It's wonderful, you put all those men together and they all see me as something different. It's what Jesus sees about me that matters. So the apostle is a man who plants and builds. He is a man who has got the prophetic edge in building something and birthing something and every Church needs that gifting. It can't be found in just one man, it never can be.

The prophet is not a man who tells you whose going to win the 3.30 at Kempton Park. The prophet isn't necessarily the person who is going to tell you what is going to happen in five years time. See, there is a difference between prophecy and being a prophet. Paul said, *I wish you all prophesied but you are not all prophets.* Prophecy: I would like to do a prophetic school one day as few people are ever taught how to use the gifts and it's so important that we learn to do that.

A lot of people come and they say, you know most of us use the gifts of the Spirit by copying other people, it's the only way we've got. So in traditional Pentecostalism you get, yea, which is the Kings James version. You can always tell by the way how people use the gifts, what version of the Bible they read. Yea, my children, yea, have I not said unto you, yea, I am your God, yea I am the Lord and yea I said unto you and the answer is yea, you're not so yea, why are you speaking like that?

You can understand if a person comes in who's not a Christian, they'll think we are a load of spiritualists listening to this. You imagine you just come in for the first time, yea, I am the Lord and I say unto you, and they think, strike, he thinks he's God. No, we are not. If we taught them they could turn round and say this, the Holy Spirit is saying this to us today, blah, blah, blah. You can test it, but if a man say's he's God, how can you test him?

See, bad teaching because there has been no teaching to know when to use the gifts. We used to be in a situation, being a good Spirit-filled Church, that as soon as the music got excited, we used to have messages in tongues going out all over the place. Every single week, every single service. Soon as Phil just paused for just one note, off it would go and it became a ritual and so we said, hang on just so, that we've prayed about the service all week and we've prayed what God wants, but we are open for Him to take another direction and we've spent a whole week praying and I've locked myself away for a day. You've rushed in, had your breakfast, come in and just liked the music and went (speaks in tongues) and you've changed the whole direction of the service just because you felt good. That's not fair fellas! If God has really has given you that, we want it but folks we have likely fasted and prayed all week for what God wanted on Sunday. Have you done the same?

So we've said, but we want it, but the Bible said and Paul said on the gifts, be they are prophetic gifts, test them, get to know them and do all these things and what you can do then if you've got a message in tongues if it can't last more than a 30 second burst, it wasn't from God. People say, well I just had to give it, I had to give it now and you'll say well why? Why is it the gift of tongues is the only gift that God can't wait? You'll burst if he doesn't give it. Of course you can wait. Well, it just goes. Well it wasn't of God then it was just a quick burst of inspiration. If it's of God you can wait 10 minutes to prophesy, you can wait ten hours to prophesy. You can wait 10 minutes to speak in tongues. It's a bit clinical. No, it's testing the gifts. It's far better to test your gift before than after because what would happen if we say I like to belong to a Church where the gifts are tested and the pastor say's, sorry you were wrong. I wouldn't go again. Alright, sit down, shut up. I wouldn't go again. So in this Church for instance, what we say, if you have got a message in tongues, unless the leaders said, now I think we've got some gifts here, let's go for it. Now, he's just released the meeting now and he's saying let's go for it, but if you feel you definitely have got a message in tongues or you have got a prophetic word, come check it with the elder and say, I just sense God's given me a tongue. We will say, OK, we're right in a very special silence at the moment, don't just wreck it, let's just wait for a moment. That's wisdom isn't it? Let's just wait on God and then you might see me sometimes go (clicks his finger) and somebody will get up and they'll speak in tongues. Then there will come an interpretation.

Then somebody says something else, somebody gives a prophetic word. Yes, that's good. You get into a habit every time you see, we used to get the traditional Pentecostalism, as soon as there was a silence (speaks in tongues). Oh, be quiet please. The poor person wasn't sensitive enough to be still and know that He was God.

That is the way you instruct. You do not quench, you instruct and then it means the person's gift then is used beautifully. They might come and say, I've got this prophetic word, blah, blah, blah and you say, actually that wasn't for the people that was for me. Thank you very much indeed, go and sit down. Now, if they had got up and thrown it over the congregation it would have confused 599 people and the pastor would have gone home saying, brilliant, I needed that Lord. Or sometimes people have come to me and I've said go give that word to that person on that row there, I counselled them this week, they'll understand what it means. Bless you. Oh, thank you.

See the reason why you've got these gifts in the Church of the prophet and you've got these gifts of the apostle, is that they actually instruct to build the Church up. That's what they are there for, not to do it all, but to teach us. To teach us how to do these things. It's terrible for judging a person for doing it wrong when nobody showed them how to do it right. They used to have schools of the prophets in the Old Testament, they did away with them somehow in the New. It's the same Holy Spirit that came upon them when they prophesied in the Old Testament as the One that came on them when they prophesied in the New Testament.

So we test the things, and if they come from God we pray over them and we say stop, hey folks, let's stop everything, here is the Word of the Lord. Beautiful isn't it? Now people feel protected then, they feel safe then. So, we believe in the prophet who comes and who said this is the Word of God now and now the prophet might then turn round and say this will happen in 2 years time.

Now prophecy is different to being a prophet. You can all prophesy and prophecy is actually not going up to somebody all the time saying don't worry, don't worry you're child's OK and God said your finances are alright. That's not necessarily prophecy. If you read the Bible you start prophesying by blessing God. Prophesy, for instance, the Lord God of Hosts, He is exalted above the nations, for He shall be worshipped so all of creation shall bow before Him and worship the Name of the Lord. That's prophecy.

See, a lot of people go straight into, I think I've got a word for you Elsie, your arthritis is going to get better in 2 days time. Now if it doesn't, she's condemned and you're confused. So if you are learning prophecy, start exalting God, once you've exalted God He will give you the rest, it comes gradually. All your gifts should start off God-ward before they become man-ward. Simple way, do it toward God and then do it toward man. If you get it right with God, you will get it right with man, but nobody teaches us this.

So as a Church we like to teach people the use of the gifts. As I have been moving for 30 years in words of knowledge, wisdom, prophecy and things like that, I don't know it all. I am still learning, but I do know a little more than most and I am so pleased to give that knowledge away so that you go on to glorify God. So we need prophets.

We need pastors, oh my goodness we need pastors. We need pastors who will care for the flock. Now, notice a pastor is not one who lords it over them, that is **Ezekiel 34.** A pastor is someone who cares and you don't have to be a preacher to be a pastor. We have got about 8 pastors in the Church and out of those maybe 3 of them preach. A pastor is a shepherd. You don't expect a shepherd sitting on a hill of Wales to be an orator and to stand there and say, to be or not to be, that is the question. We'll be noble in the mind, slings and arrows and all this. No, a pastor is a person who binds up the broken hearted, cares for them, looks for the lost sheep. They are in lambing and knock 7 bells out of the foxes and wolves. Sometimes they are just an ordinary rough man with rough hands and a cap and a dog and a whistle. You know, we often say, I want to be a pastor and sit in a nice office and wear a lovely suit. Well I'll tell you folks there are not many of them about. To be a pastor often means you lay your life down, always means you lay your life down for the sheep.

We need the evangelist. The one who evokes the Gospel, the one who provokes us to the Gospel who says, don't sit in, get out, share your faith. Come on now, be a witness. We say, it must be wonderful to be an evangelist. Well, no his job actually is to bring us to the point where we are an evangel.

Now the Bible says the pastors must be apt to teach, elders must be apt to teach, which means they must be able to give a reason for the hope that's within them, but we do believe in the gift of teachers who have a specific gift of teaching the truths of the Word of God.

Now some men and women can have overlaps of some of those gifts, but they are distinct gifts. They called Jesus a prophet, they called Him the Son of God. So we believe in gifts in the Church.

We believe in deacons. Deacons are the ones we believe who are men full of the Holy Ghost who will do the practical things. Our deacons in this Church do not sit in government, they sit in servanthood. They take care of the building, they take care of the widows, they distribute the finance to people in need, but they are not in a rulership position. We have elders, we have pastors, we have deacons, we have trustees and deacons are the men full of the Holy Ghost and what they do is they wait on tables. So we don't vote them in, we don't vote anybody into this Church, it's not a dictatorship, but then again it's not a democracy, because a democracy is not in the Bible. What we say is, here is a man we are considering being an elder, we have investigated his position. If anybody here knows of any reason why Biblically he should not be one, please let us know in 10 days. So it means that if the man is not Biblically sound, is not a good witness at work, he's not a good witness at home and he hasn't got his home in order, you have the Divine right to tell us if we've missed something. If not, we don't vote on him because he is a nice man and gives out sweets. So we do value everybody's input into this fellowship, but when it comes to the giftings and the leadership we never have votes and we never have a seconder and nobody puts their hands up with a majority. Sheep don't vote in shepherds. Never have done. It's not Biblical, but every sheep should report the shepherd if he misuses them, or abuses them, or is not living a Godly life. So, that is just the way we operate. We are not a dictatorship, we are not a democracy. We try to be theocracy, we try to hear the Voice of God and go with Him and nobody in our Church is there forever. If we feel their gifting changes and we are quite open to go in and do that.

Now I could say far more on the ministry of the Church and gifts in the Church but we are going to leave it there and you can discuss anything else with a pastor.

What Is A Disciple In The Kingdom Of God? What Do We Really Want You To Be If You Are Part Of This Fellowship, Because Our Job Is To Expose The Gift Inside You?

The Bible says He gives unto His people gifts and the idea is that we use those gifts and just like the fruit that is part of us, it is multiplied. Now gifts come into two categories, the category of natural gifting and spiritual gifting. Sometimes because we feel the gift is natural, we can't use it for God. I have seen people who are just brilliant keyboard players, and say, I was just good at music, I can't use that for God, the answer is, of course you can. You bring it, you sanctify it, and you use it.

There is a Scripture that says, **Whatever you find in your hand to do, do it with all your might.** So if a man is an accountant, gifted in making money, he doesn't have to have a spiritual gift, he can take the one that God has birthed in Him and he can have it sanctified and use it for God. If a man was a millionaire before he became a Christian, so long as what he is doing is ethical and righteous, then he doesn't have to have an apostolic gift put on his hands, he can go and make another million for the kingdom of God. Because there are natural giftings within us, your parents could be musical, you could be musical, they could be intellectual, and you could be intellectual. They can be sporty, you could be sporty. Some of it is passed down through natural genes, other gifts are given by God.

Supernaturally God gives you these gifts and you have the ability to counsel, or you have wisdom, or whatever. These gifts are from God. The Bible says, if any man lacks wisdom let him ask of God and He gives it liberally and He holds nothing back. So we have different gifting; people say we are not a large church, according to anything like what is going on in the world, but sadly in our nation we are quite sizeable. People say if you join a bigger church, you are just a number and you will never have opportunity to use your gifting. I reverse that; the reason we are a big church is because everyone's giftings are open to be used. Our job is to sort it, set it in it's right place, so that we can see you bless God and bless the people. So whatever gift you have, unless it is an obscure one, like pigeon hunting in Outer Mongolia, I am sure - and even if that was it - we would seek to put you in touch with a pigeon fancier in that country.

So we do believe in Discipleship. A disciple is a disciplined learner and the problem is that in Christianity, so many Christians are known for their indiscipline. Indiscipline in their prayer life, their daily life, in their witnessing and in their giving. We see so much of this in the church in our nation at the moment, a bit like the children of Israel when they were in Egypt. Their prayers were going up to God, but they were imprisoned by the things of this world: we too need to be liberated from the Egypt spirit.

Whereby we live by circumstances - the Bible tells us to be overcomers. An overcomer is greater than an undertaker, you know if you are always under the circumstances then your best friend is the undertaker. But if you are over the circumstances, your best friend is the overcomer. And I would much rather be part of the overcomers than the undertakers, because one ends up in the box and the other opening the box.

As a church and as a fellowship here we would like you to become a disciple of Jesus Christ. Now God's command was **to go and make disciples,** that is a command, so everyone is called to do that. How does that happen?

It is important that we witness. Witness is not having a degree in evangelism, it is knowing that we have been changed by God and allowing the change to ooze out. In fact to be a witness is to be like toothpaste and let God squeeze you. Every time some one squeezes us, God should ooze out. We should be a witness. The Bible says, **You will be a witness when the Holy Spirit comes upon you,** not you will learn to be.

Today I went out to get a sandwich from a shop round the corner. They know I am a Pastor and I chat with them and pray and sing. Today I went to get my sandwich and they said, stay and have it with us. So I sat down and they brought me a plate. I said I would have a can of pop, then they brought a glass, then a napkin. I sat there talking whilst they were serving and they said they would like to put up posters now of the church. They wanted to know what we believe and everything else. This was just from talking. **You shall be a witness when the Holy Ghost comes upon you.** Witnessing is wonderful - you know it is like being a taxi with "For Hire" on it. All the taxi does is just park where the people are and they say, "Taxi!" The taxi driver goes all red and embarrassed, I didn't like to admit I'm a taxi. No, taxi drivers wait for fares. Witnessing - often some of the most fruitful - is where you go where the people are and say, God I'm available. Surprising how many people come up and say, excuse me are you going where I am going? You say, No, are you going where I am going?

We believe every one can be a witness. If you are at college, you can be a witness by the way you work. If you are at the home, you can witness in the way you react. So it is important that we witness. We believe there are practical steps for fulfilling the commission of God, we do believe in the power of the Spirit, but also the power of understanding.

We believe in praying. Prayer is not one-way, but it is, **be still and know that I am God.** Sometimes, we have to be still and allow God to speak to us. Some of the most dramatic times are when God speaks to us. You say, David, how does God speak? Some say a quiet voice, a mighty rushing wind, sometimes He gives you a Scripture and you look it up. One I often give was - because it was dramatic in my life - on September 2nd 1997. I had a heart attack in the car on my way to London. I was admitted into Solihull hospital, in intensive care, all dripped up. I just said, Lord, I don't know what to say to you, Lord, if You are calling me to go home. At that time my eldest son was 14 and my daughter was 11 and the youngest 4. I said, Lord, I don't want to lose these my children, but if You are calling me home, I am not going to struggle, for some reason if this is time to go. If I am getting in Your way, or something else, Lord, I just want to know.

So I just lay there and suddenly in the stillness God said, look up **Revelation 2:10** and the Bible said, **"Do not worry when these things come upon you because Satan will bring some of you to prison and some to the point of death but in 10 days I will give you a glorious future".** I shut the Bible and I looked over to the nurse, she asked if I was in pain, I said, no, but do you know how long I am going to be in here? She said, yes, it is mandatory, 10 days. I smiled and she said, what is it? I said, nothing and said, goodnight. I knew I was going to be kept, so I just snuggled down and went to sleep.

You see prayer is not like going to Tesco's and saying, have I got my list? It is immature, it is like talking to Father Christmas, excuse me Father I want to sit on your knee and tell you the 16 things I want for Christmas. Instead, it is wonderful and first of all exalts who He is. The Bible says, **pray without ceasing but rejoice evermore.** You have prayer, rejoicing and in the middle is the Word. It is a bit like a sandwich; a sandwich is not a sandwich without the bread, but not a sandwich without anything in the middle. A sandwich is two things pressed together. Prayer and praise surrounding the Word make a man whole. A man who has got the Word inside of him and prayer and praise either side of him is a man who is beautifully sandwiched with God. We want you to learn to pray without ceasing, so part of your prayer is exalting, part of your prayer is asking and part of your prayer is hearing.

All through Revelation John says, **Jesus said Hear what the Spirit is saying to the Church.** And, of course, we, like the disciples, say, **teach us how to pray,** because no one knows how to pray, we are still learning. Praying is communicating with the heart of God from the heart of man. We want this to be a praying Church. We have about 5 prayer meetings a week and as we get toward a move of God in our nation that will increase.

We have a men's prayer meeting and a ladies' prayer meeting. We have a general prayer meeting, then we have specialised prayer meetings all over the place. We now have a Prayer Tower, if you visit that it is on the outside of the building with a small staircase, it will be open. We are looking this year to have it open 7 days a week, morning, noon and night, where we are going to be praying for the whole of the area and we will have people interceding and praying for the people 24 hours a day. It is our own Prayer Tower, it was given by God in the most miraculous way, which we will tell you about if you ask us some time.

We believe in giving and doing. Both giving of our time, our substance, we believe tithing and money is not just an Old Testament law, it is something that existed before that. Tithing came before the law and we do believe that God talks about First Fruits. Paul puts it this way, on the first day of the week lay something on one side for God. Now of course, if Christianity has freed you from the bondage of the law, then there is no way a Christian should give less than a legal Jew. A legal Jew used to give ten per cent of all of his income to God. Now if we are under the new covenant of Grace and not Law, surely then the minimum we should give is ten per cent? Well people say, we are free from all that now and I don't believe in tithing. People who don't believe in tithing are the people who don't give anything. Because if a man gives anything, why should he worry about ten per cent if he is giving 50% or 40%? It is a natural thing, God says to bring unto Me your first fruits. Another person who had a big problem with tithing was Cain and he wanted to justify what he was bringing, but we need to bring our first fruits, I don't care if you call it tithing, love giving, or whatever, you give it. God said I want your first fruits and so we do believe that as we give unto God this Church is very blessed and enabled to bless missionaries. We've just started another fund now where we are trusting to give £25,000 a year away on top of what we give now to missions and God is good, all the time.

As we give, we do not give to get, but as we give of the seed, God returns the harvest. It's not just money, it's time, it's attitude. We believe God wants the first fruits of all our life. People say, how can I tithe time, there is only 24 hours in a day? It's quite easy, you put God first in your time and I found when I was in business I could do more business in 3 days than men in the world did in 6. See God multiplies your time, He doesn't give you more than 24 hours, but if you give God your time and you find what it takes a man a day to do, you can do in 2 hours. God gives His people favour. He's a great God, all the time. We believe in praying, giving and going. So on to another fundamental area.

Experience. Testimony grows out of experience of Christ. The Holy Spirit enhances our experience. We do not live purely an experiential life, but we do know that we've seen Jesus, that we've had an experience of His love. Never be frightened to say, **I speak that which I do know.**

Assurance. To be a disciple we expect you to grow in assurance, which is confidence building between God and believer. The hymn writer said, Blessed assurance, Jesus is mine, what a foretaste of glory divine. There is nothing worse than seeing a Christian who doesn't know what they believe. Paul said, **I know whom I have believed and**

I am persuaded that he is able to keep which I have committed against that day. There is a difference between presumption, assumption and assurance. Presumption is because I've read, I've got to have it. Assurance is by God's grace I've got it. It's by God's grace. Grace means God's favour.

Boldness. Early Christians acted with boldness and they made an impression. Boldness is not rudeness. Boldness is not arrogance. As one programme said, we boldly go where no Christian has ever been before. Boldness means courage, God given courage. We want to see in this Church people who are not wimps, but people who can stand - of all dispositions, sex and creed - and who can say, you know I am immovable by God's grace; **having done all** said the Scripture **to stand.** Knowing that if He's given us the call, He's given us the ability. We do have it.

The Bible said, **be of good courage, I have overcome the world.** Now if God said, **be of good courage,** who knows we can be! We believe that Christians should be discipled to be people of understanding and not be tossed hither and thither with words of doctrine. We should start where we are and work from there. We should concentrate on the experience already given by God, build on the precepts, forget not His benefits. You know people can see that there has been a change in our life. We should become people of the Word, we should become people who read the Word. It's surprising how many people own one (a Bible), just like something under an aeroplane that we only use in times of emergency. This is not a life jacket in case the plane goes down, this is something that keeps the plane up. This is the Word of God that keeps us in heavenly places. David said, **thy Word have I hid in my heart so then I won't sin against You.** Jesus said in **John 15**, My Words live inside you. That's powerful, I preached this the other Sunday, and He said, My Words live inside you. Then He said, whatever you ask in My Name I'll give it you. A lot of people are very disillusioned and they say, I've asked God and He's not given it me. But hang on, are they the things that Jesus would have asked for? If the answer is no, that's why. He said, My Words have I put in your heart so that whatever you ask you will get. Now, isn't that wonderful because Jesus even knows what we should ask for. And that is why the Holy Spirit said, when we get to the point with our groanings we do not know what to ask for, the Holy Spirit intercedes knowing what we should ask for. That's great isn't it? You know somebody said if a genie came and said 3 wishes you wouldn't know what to give. If Jesus comes and asks for a wish we still do not know what to give, but the Holy Spirit knows because He searches the heart of God and the heart of man. Is that good or good?

We expect and we would like to see Christians grow to have a capability; the gifts of the Holy Spirit make us capable to make disciples. We speak with wisdom and insight. God's given us the ability. We would like to see Christians with the opportunity; see the Holy Spirit gives initiative. The Spirit leads men and women. Do you know you'll always be given an opportunity in this Church. We might find that what you'll think your gifting is, we find it different. Whoever does anything in this fellowship is on only a year's contract, be they full or part time, because we find that by giving somebody a one year contract, if at the end of that time they feel they shouldn't be in Faith Builders, children's work, some people feel so offended and embarrassed that they leave Church because they don't like to say, I want to step down from a gift. We say, work for a year and at the end of that time, if you have fulfilled your contract, well done thou good and faithful servant, now let's see if you should be in music, or should you be in something else and release you to something else. Some people feel that because they are in a ministry, they have got to be in it till the day they die and the answer is no, things change folks. We might see it as a need that you grow into something else, so there is an opportunity in discipleship.

Love. Show the love of Christ. Few people can resist the impact of love. God is a God who loves.

We disciple Christians at the moment in many ways, Church meetings, house or home-link groups, nurture, Alpha groups and one-to-one discipleship. We should have a hunger for God, a thirst for the Holy living. There should be a desire to a greater knowledge of God. We have a Bible School. Be committed to the Lordship of Jesus in your lives, wanting His will on every matter, no matter what it costs to have a desire to be used of God.

Have a love for God and for all His people. Be filled with the Holy Spirit; you say, wow, this is heavy. No, this is releasing. How should disciples behave? They should communicate, join in enthusiastically in Christ. They shouldn't go around miserable and moaning. They should show the unconditional sacrificial love of God and go the extra mile. Be readily available, helping by giving up time and energy to help people. Giving their finances, sharing their lives and their homes with people; pray, pray, pray as people come to mind. Challenge to even greater faith and commitment. Encourage people with potential, express appreciation and nurture improvements in people. They should set Godly goals - always being on time, stopping bad habits, never doing anything that can cause another to stumble. Giving time, talent, resources and extending the Kingdom of God.

WEEK 6
HOLY COMMUNION

Why should we take Communion?

What is the significance of the bread and the wine in Holy Communion?

Communion itself is one of the 2 great ordinances of the Christian faith, water baptism being the other, and is practised to some degree by all major Christian denominations, being known as the Lord's Table, or Holy Eucharist, as well as Communion and the Sacrament.

The Anglican and Catholic churches offer the opportunity for all believers to partake in Communion on a daily basis, reflecting the practise of the early church.

Acts 2:46   *"So continuing daily with one accord in the temple, and breaking bread from house to house, they ate their food with gladness and simplicity of heart".*

In some churches only ordained ministers are allowed to administer the Eucharist, often performing ritualistic blessing of the emblems before offering them to the congregation, whilst in others congregations informally share amongst themselves.

The bread shared varies from a supermarket loaf to specially prepared communion 'wafers', with wine being anything from specially prepared and fermented communion wine to non-alcoholic versions such as given in the Methodist church, or to the 'Ribena' substitute common in charismatic churches.

Whilst any of the above can cause discussion and debate, it rarely creates a reason not to participate, unlike the accepted doctrines of the Catholic and Lutheran churches. Roman Catholics believe in "transubstantiation", i.e. that the bread and wine supernaturally and physically become the flesh and blood of Jesus when taken in Holy Communion. On the other hand, Martin Luther proposed "consubstantiation", i.e. that although the bread and wine do not alter physically, they call into being the physical presence of Christ's flesh and blood. However, nowadays both of these doctrines are rejected by most Protestant denominations.

However, we will discount the physical role of the bread and wine in the act of Holy Communion, and ask the reader to accept the symbolic nature of the act and instead concentrate on the spiritual dimensions of The Sacrament.

The Emblems

Firstly, then, we will look at the nature of the bread and then the wine, before looking at why we should partake of them in communion. The first mention we have of bread and wine is in the Book of Genesis, when Melchidezek, who is a type (or example/illustration) of Christ, meets Abram.

> *Genesis 14:18*   *"Then Melchizedek king of Salem brought out bread and wine; he was the priest of God Most High".*

Many Bible commentators believe that God intended that Melchidezek, as Priest and King, should provide an order of which Jesus would be the only practitioner. If this is so, then clearly He intended that the bread and wine should be recognised as instruments of the blessing He bestowed upon Abraham.

The Bread

To understand the significance of the bread, we need to look at the part bread played in God's picture in the history of atonement and how Jesus related Himself to that.

Although bread in the Old Testament often symbolised abundance of blessing as a result of good harvests, we first see it given a symbolic role by God in the celebration of the Passover.

> *Exodus 12:17-20*   *"So you shall observe the Feast of Unleavened Bread, for on this same day I will have brought your armies out of the land of Egypt. Therefore you shall observe this day throughout your generations as an everlasting ordinance. In the first month, on the fourteenth day of the month at evening, you shall eat unleavened bread, until the twenty-first day of the month at evening. For seven days no leaven shall be found in your houses, since whoever eats what is leavened, that same person shall be cut off from the congregation of Israel, whether he is a stranger or a native of the land. You shall eat nothing leavened; in all your habitations you shall eat unleavened bread".*

God establishes an act of remembrance of the covenant He has made with Israel. The absence of leaven (yeast) is significant, because God is demonstrating once again the need for Israel to be holy, set apart from the nations around them, not subject to other influences which can alter the nature of their worship and relationship with God.

That act of remembrance was extended, when in order to sustain the Israelites in the wilderness, God provided them with Manna.

Exodus 16:32　*"Then Moses said, 'This is thing which the LORD has commanded: 'Fill an omer with it, to be kept for your generations, that they may see the bread with which I fed you to in the wilderness, when I brought you out of the land of Egypt'".*

That bread was to form part of the ritual God instigated in the Tabernacle and Temple for atonement.

Exodus 25:30　*"And you shall set the showbread on the table before Me always".*

Significantly, whilst many of the offerings included bread made with yeast, the bread utilised by the priests had to be unleavened.

Right at the beginning of His earthly ministry, Jesus confirms this view of Himself.

Matthew 4:3-4　*"Now when the tempter came to Him, he said, 'If You are the Son of God, command that these stones become bread'. But He answered and said, 'It is written, Man shall not live by bread alone, but by every word that proceeds from the mouth of God'".*

Jesus is of course The Word *(John 1:1+14)* and therefore proclaimed that He was the very Manna the Israelites had come to believe the awaited Messiah would provide.

John 6:31-35　*"Our fathers ate the manna in the desert; as it is written: He gave them bread from heaven to eat. Then Jesus said to them, 'Most assuredly, I say to you, Moses did not give you the bread from heaven, but My Father gives you the true bread from heaven. For the bread of God is He who comes down from heaven and gives life to the world'. Then they said to Him, 'Lord, give us this bread always'. And Jesus said to them, "I am the bread of life. He who comes to Me shall never hunger, and he who believes in Me shall never thirst'".*

John 6:48-51　*"I am the bread of life. Your fathers ate the manna in the wilderness, and are dead. Bu this is the bread which comes down from heaven, that one may eat of it and not die. I am the living bread which came down from heaven. If anyone eats of this bread, he will live forever; and the bread that I shall give is My flesh, which I shall give for the life of the world".*

This was a teaching the disciples literally found hard to swallow, and it constantly became a stumbling block to them as they failed to recognize the significance of the breaking of bread in the feeding of the multitudes, or Jesus' teaching on the need to beware the yeast of the Pharisees and Sadducees.

It was on the first day of the Feast of Unleavened Bread that Jesus met with the disciples for the Passover. Then He, the Paschal Lamb of God, established His lasting ordnance of remembrance.

Luke 22:19 *"And He took bread, gave thanks and broke it, and gave it to them, saying, 'This is My body which is given for you; do this in remembrance of Me'".*

Finally, the 'daily bread' Jesus asks us to request from the Father is not the physical bread the Jews anticipated, but the spiritual food of Jesus which we will partake of when He returns to establish His Kingdom, which is our proclamation.

1 Corinthians 11:26 *"For as often as you eat this bread and drink this cup, you proclaim the Lord's death till He comes".*

Revelation 2:17 *"... To him who overcomes, I will give some of the hidden manna to eat ...".*

The Blood

Having followed through the Old and New Testament to look at the bread, let us now backtrack from the Last Supper to examine the significance of the wine.

Luke 22:20 *"Likewise He also took the cup after supper, saying, 'This cup is the new covenant in My blood, which is shed for you'".*

Jesus was demonstrating to the disciples that which He had already taught, but had not been understood by them.

John 6:52-64 *"The Jews therefore quarrelled among themselves, saying 'How can this Man give us His flesh to eat?' Then Jesus said to them, 'Most assuredly, I say to you, unless you eat the flesh of the Son of Man and drink His blood, you have no life in you. Whoever eats My flesh and drinks My blood has eternal life, and I will raise him up at the last day. For My flesh is food indeed, and My blood is drink indeed. He who eats My flesh and drinks My blood abides in Me, and I in him. As the living Father sent Me, and I live because of the Father, so he who feeds on Me will live* *because of Me. This is the bread which came down from heaven - not as your fathers ate the manna, and are dead. He who eats this bread will live forever'. These things He said in the synagogue as He taught in Capernaum. Therefore many of His disciples, when they heard this, said, 'This is a hard saying; who can understand it?' When Jesus knew in Himself that His disciples murmured about this, He said to them, 'Does this offend you? What then if you see the Son of Man ascend where He was before? It is the Spirit who gives life; the flesh profits nothing. The words that I speak to you are spirit, and they are life. But there are some of you who do not believe ...".*

It is only in the spiritual that we can see the true meaning of Jesus' words and these are demonstrated in the Book of Revelation as revealed to John in the Spirit.

Revelation 12:11 *"And they overcame him by the blood of the Lamb and by the word of their testimony ...".*

Revelation 5:9 *"... You are worthy to take the scroll, and to open its seals; for You were slain, and You have redeemed us to God by Your blood out of every tribe and tongue and people and nation ...'".*

Here we see clearly demonstrated the significance of the shedding of blood by the Lamb of God. That picture was one with which the Jews were all too familiar and was referred to consistently by the Gospel writers.

Centuries before, during the Passover, God had established the sprinkling of blood as a means of averting God's wrath.

Exodus 12:22-23 *"And you shall take a bunch of hyssop, dip it in the blood that is in the basin, and strike the lintel and the two doorposts with the blood that is in the basin. And none of you shall go out of the door of his house until morning. For the LORD will pass through to strike the Egyptians; and when He sees the blood on the lintel and on the two doorposts, the LORD will pass over the door and not allow the destroyer to come into your houses to strike you".*

Jesus described Himself as the door, and His blood became the atonement for our sins. He talked of His 'Blood of the new covenant', reflecting the words of Moses to the Israelites.

Exodus 24:8 *"And Moses took the blood, sprinkled it on the people,* and said, 'Behold, the blood of the covenant which the LORD has made with you according to all these words'".

Matthew 26:28 "For this is My blood of the new covenant, which is shed for many for the remission of sins".

The priests themselves were purified for service to the Lord by the applying of the blood of the sacrifice to their earlobe, thumb and toe representing a covering in blood. That need for a covering was established in the Garden when God clothed Adam and Eve with the skins of animals.

The need for blood sacrifice was recognised by Abel, and Jesus' blood became the all-atoning sacrifice for the sin of Man. The writer of **Hebrews** goes to great lengths to make the connection in **chapter 10** and also:

Hebrews 12:24 "To Jesus the Mediator of the new covenant, and to the blood of sprinkling that speaks better things than that of Abel".

The whole of the history of God's people points to the blood of Jesus as man's means of atonement.

1 Peter 1:18-20 "Knowing that you were not redeemed with corruptible things, like silver or gold, from your aimless conduct received from your fathers, but with the precious blood of Christ, as of a lamb without blemish and without spot. He indeed was foreordained before the foundation of the world, but was manifest in these last times for you".

The Communion

Exodus 23:18 "You shall not offer the blood of My sacrifice with leavened bread ...".

Jesus cannot do anything contrary to the Word of God, and therefore in offering up His Body as the Bread of Life, then He had to be without sin in His flesh.

Likewise therefore as an act of Covenant, we too must ensure we approach the act of communion in a worthy manner.

1 Corinthians 11:27-29 "Therefore whoever eats this bread or drinks this cup of the Lord in an unworthy manner will be guilty of the body and blood of the Lord. But let a man examine himself, and so let him eat of that bread and drink of that cup. For he who eats and drinks in an unworthy manner eats and drinks judgment to himself, not discerning the

Lord's body".

In summary, the partaking of the Bread and Wine has a number of significances.

As a legacy, being part of Christ's last Will and Testament and as a memorial, being commanded as an act of remembrance of the sacrifice and substitution Christ made for our sins.

1 Corinthians 11:24 "And when He had given thanks, He broke it and said, 'Take, eat; this is My body which is broken for you; do this in remembrance of Me'".

As a proclamation of our oneness with Christ and denouncement of the enemy.

1 Corinthians 10:21 "You cannot drink the cup of the Lord and the cup of demons; you cannot partake of the Lord's table and of the table of demons".

As a prophetic act of witness.

1 Corinthians 11:26 "For as often as you eat this bread and drink this cup, you proclaim the Lord's death till He comes".

As a means of examining ourselves and our relationship with God and others, for we are partakers of the act of covenant described above.

As an act of thanksgiving and obedience, for this is a command of Jesus- **"Do this in remembrance of Me".** In partaking in the Lord's Supper we must discern who He is, what He has done, what He has accomplished on our behalf, and what His promise holds for us. We abide in Christ when we do His will, in embracing the act of Communion and it's true spiritual significance, we will be reminded of what the fullness of "do this in remembrance of Me" means, and receive the continued power to live out the life Christ requires of us.

John 6: 54-56   *"Whoever eats My flesh and drinks My blood has eternal life, and I will raise him up at the last day. For My flesh is food indeed and My blood is drink indeed. He who eats My flesh and drinks My blood abides in Me, and I in him"*.

* *

The Leadership Structure of Renewal Christian Centre

Most of those in leadership at Renewal operate on a voluntary, part-time basis; those who are full-time paid workers are indicated below by bold lettering.

This information is correct as of June 2005.

Senior Pastor

Pastor David Carr, and his wife Molly, were called by the Lord to start Renewal in August 1972; he has been the Senior Pastor even since. Responsible for the vision and the spiritual direction of the Church in co-operation with the Elders. Leader of the pastoral and administrative departments of the Family Centre and Conference Centre, giving advice to the senior leaders of all departments. Regional Overseer, Midlands area, of the Free Methodist Church and is also responsible for planting churches throughout the UK.

Assistant Pastor

Richard Taylor came to Renewal in 2000 and was appointed Assistant Pastor in 2004; as such he serves as Pastor David's deputy. Responsible for leading the teams that plan and implement the Ministry of Power missions.

Chief Executive

Jim Ogden gives leadership in administration and finance for the maintenance and provision of the facilities at the central Church and the satellites.

Senior Pastor's Office

Responsible for the day-to-day spiritual and pastoral work of the Church. Comprises **Richard Taylor,** Assistant Pastor; **Matt Spina,** who is responsible not just for the youth of the Church but also networks with schools and other organisations in the region; **Justin Marsh,** who oversees the pastoral needs of the Church, the teams of Area Deacons, partnership applications, hospital and home visits, weddings, funerals and baptisms; & **Tim Uluirewa,** who is Pastor of Worship and Media of the Central Church and satellites.

Church Office

Supports the Chief Executive in the day-to-administration of the Church.

Elders

Give spiritual advice and guidance to the Senior Pastor. Comprise Niall Cluley, David Russell, Rob Williams, **Richard Taylor** & Phil Lane.

Pastoral Care Team

Assist the Senior Pastor's Office in the day-to-day care and support of Partners and attenders. Comprise Tony Carr, Malcolm Beamond, Ian Coley, Peter Earle, John Hawker, Simon Hodges, Ben Lees, Anne Lowe, Tony Matthews, Chris Oyede, Nick Pearson, Gary Spencer, Rory Thompson, David Tompkins & John Watkinson.

Satellite Leaders

Renewal comprises not only a central Church, located in Lode Lane, but a number of satellite Churches around the Heart of England. Each of these satellites holds their own Sunday evening services, as well as various other meetings during the week. Each Satellite is headed by its own leader, namely:

- o Alcester - Simon Hodges
- o Birmingham - Chris Oyede
- o Chelmsley Wood - Tony Matthews & Nick Pearson
- o Coventry - Peter Earle
- o Lichfield - Malcolm Beamond
- o Redditch - Ian Coley
- o Stratford - John Hawker
- o Warwick & Leamington - Ben Lees

Trustees

Legally responsible for the finances and all the property and buildings. Comprise **David Carr,** Niall Cluley, Roger Wragg, Tony Burchell, Geoff Greenaway, Chris Towler, Phil Greenaway & Andy Earles.

Area Deacons

Support the pastors in providing day-to-day care and support for the Partners and attenders. In order to find out the names of your local Area Deacon please contact the Church Office (0121 711 7300).

Contacting the Church

For:

- o "Everyday" concerns please contact the Church Office (9.30 - 5.00 Monday - Friday) on 0121 711 7300.

- o Emergency Pastoral Care (when the Church Office is closed) - 07768 084268.

- o The Church website go to ***www.renewalcc.com***

Denomination

The Church is a member of the Free Methodist Church (UK Conference).